Vukovar

Both Sides Now
Sa obje strane
Са обје стране

Twenty years later, war and
postwar stories from one Balkan town.

Linda Garrett
Sandra Marić

VUKOVAR
Both Sides Now
Twenty Years Later: War and Postwar Stores from One Balkan Town

Cover Design: Leslie Carlson
Photography: Linda Garrett
Editing and Layout: Laura Kelly

ISBN-10:
1463554176

ISBN-13:
978-1463554170

www.vukovarbothsidesnow.com

THE END AND THE BEGINNING

Wislawa Szymborska*

After every war
Someone has to tidy up.
Things won't pick
Themselves up, after all.

Someone has to shove
The rubble to the roadside
So the carts loaded with corpses
Can get by.

Someone has to trudge
Through sludge and ashes,
Through the sofa springs
The shards of glass,
The bloody rags.

Someone has to lug the post
To prop the wall,
Someone has to glaze the windows,
Set the door in its frame.

No sound bites,
No photo opportunities
And it takes years.
All the cameras have gone
To other wars.

The bridges need to be rebuilt,
The railroad stations too.
Shirtsleeves will be rolled
To shreds.

Someone, broom in hand,
Still remembers how it was
Someone else listens, nodding
His unshattered head.

But others are bound
To be bustling nearby
Who'll find all that
A little boring.

From time to time someone still must
Dig up a rusted armament
From underneath a bush
And haul it off to the dump.

Those who knew
What this was all about
Must make way
For those who knew little
And less than that.
And at last nothing less than nothing.

Someone must lie there
In the grass that covers up
The causes and effects
With a corn stalk in his teeth
Gawking at clouds.

*Polish Poet and Nobel Prize Winner 2006

CONTENTS

CONTENTS (continued)

GLOSSARY

Borovo: *Suburb of Vukovar. Home of Borovo Factory that employed some 25,000 people from 24 ethnic groups until economic collapse in 1980s.*

Borovo Selo: *Suburb of Vukovar.*

Četniks: *Serb nationalist movement founded in late 19th century; fought against Communist Partisans in World War II; name also used as disparaging term for all Serb paramilitaries during 1991-1995 war.*

Defenders: *Croat armed defenders of Vukovar, most civilian, from August-November 1991*

Glavaš, Branimir: *HDZ leader; commander of ZNG in Osijek region; accused of war crimes*

HDZ: *Hrvatska Demokratska Zajednica, Croatian Democratic Union*

HOS: *Hrvatske Odbrambene Snage, Croatian Defense Force, military wing of HSP*

HSP: *Hrvatska Stranka Prava, Croatian Party of Rights*

ICRC: *International Committee of the Red Cross*

ICTY: *International Criminal Tribunal for the Former Yugoslavia*

JNA: *Jugoslavenska Narodna Armija, Yugoslav Peoples' Army*

Krajina: *Established by Austrians as military barrier to the Ottoman Empire; territory disputed by Croatia and Serbia; "Republica Srpska Krajina" declared in 1991 by local Serbs.*

Milosević, Slobodan: *President of Socialist Republic of Serbia, Republic of Serbia and then the Federal Republic of Yugoslavia - from 1997-2000; indicted by ICTY in 2001, died in The Hague in 2006 of natural causes.*

MUP: *Ministarstvo unutrasnjih poslova (Ministry of internal affairs) Croatian special police units formed after 1990 elections in Croatia*

Ovčara: *Pig farm located south of Vukovar; site of execution and burial of some 200 defenders, hospital workers,wounded, and journalists on November 19-20, 1991.*

PHR: *Physicians for Human Rights, organized exhumation of Ovčara grave*

Radio Dunav: *Serb radio station in Vukovar; founded in December 1991 after fall of Vukovar as first civilian institution in the town*

Hrvatski Radio Vukovar:
Croat radio; only source of information during the siege of the town; journalist Sinisa Glavasević was the "voice" of Vukovar until November 18, 1991 and was executed at Ovčara.

RSK: *Republica Srpska Krajina*

SDP: *Stranka Demokratskih Promjena, Part of Democratic Change (reformed Communist Party)*

SDS: *Srpska Demokratska Stranka, Serbian Democratic Party in Croatia*

Šešelj, Vojislav: *Serbian ultranationalist leader, commander of paramilitary unit*

SCIC: *Serbian Council Information Center*

Sljivančanin, Major Veselin:
JNA officer responsible for breaking agreement with ICRC on protection of wounded, of hospital workers, civilians, prisoners of war.

Slavonija: *Region of Croatia; Eastern Slavonia is the region along the Croat-Serb border with the Danube as the frontier between the two countries*

Sremska Mitrovica:
Site of concentration camp for Croat prisoners, in Vojvodina Serbia

TO: *Teritorijalna Odbrana, Territorial Defense, local defense units*

Tuđjman, Franjo: *Founder and leader of HDZ, first president of independent Croatia*

UNPROFOR: *United Nations Protection Force*

UNTAES: *United Nations Transitional Authority Eastern Slavonia*

Ustaša: *World War II fascist movement; also disparaging name for all Croat nationalists*

Velepromet: *Warehouse complex in a suburb of Vukovar (near Ovčara); holding center for Croats from Vukovar after the fall of the town.*

Vojvodina: *Autonomous region of Yugoslavia on Serb side of the Danube*

ZNG: *Zbor Narodne Garde , Croatian National Guard, precursor to Croatian Army*

VUKOVAR WAR CHRONOLOGY

1990   Yugoslavia begins to crumble as Slovenia and Croatia initiate separation process. In April Croatia holds first democratic elections. Franjo Tuđjman of the nationalist HDZ party is elected president.

1991   May 1, 2: The explosive events in the village of Borovo Selo near Vukovar are still in dispute twenty years later. This marks the beginning of the war for some people.

End of May: As tensions rise, Vukovar's Serb parents send their children east across the Danube to Serbia at end of school year.

June 25: Croatia declares independence.

August 4: Busloads of Croat women and children evacuate west to the coast.

August 24: First aerial attack against Vukovar by the JNA air force; JNA tanks move in from the south; 25,000 people still in town.

September 19: JNA surrounds Vukovar and digs in for a two-month siege and bombardment. Hundreds of men organize defense of the town and of the civilian population taking refuge in basements.

November 18: Vukovar's defenders negotiate surrender to the JNA; survivors leave shelters after three months to see the town destroyed; buildings on fire, bodies in the streets. Some 5-6000 people are marched to the cemetery; men and women are separated and loaded on busses; defenders surrender weapons and are taken to concentration camps in Serbia; women and children are released to Croat authorities days later.

November 19: At 1:00 am the JNA enters the hospital ahead of the ICRC monitors in violation of surrender agreement. JNA Major Veselin Sljivančanin prohibits ICRC officials from entering the hospital; unsupervised forced evacuation begins as JNA and paramilitaries remove hundreds of men, ages 16-60; they are loaded on busses and driven first to JNA barracks in Vukovar and then to the Ovčara pig farm where they are beaten by Serb paramilitaries; at 6 pm the men are divided into groups of about 20, loaded into trucks and taken away.

A total of 264 men – wounded, fighters, hospital workers and journalists are executed at Ovčara during the night of November 19th- 20th.

December: Eighteen Serbs and one Hungarian tortured and executed in Paulin Dvor, near Vukovar, by Croats.

1992   January 15: EU and US recognize independence of Croatia.

February 26: Slavonia incorporated into 'Republic of Serbian Krajina'

1993   May: International Criminal Tribunal for Yugoslavia (ICTY) created.

December: UNTAES (United Nations Transitional Authority for Easter Slavonia) arrives in Vukovar

1995   August 4-8: Croatian army launches Operation Storm; it is not extended to Eastern Slavonia, the only region in Croatia left with a Serb population after the war.

November 12: Erdut Agreement is signed between Croat authorities and eastern Krajina Serbs on peaceful reintegration of the region, including Vukovar.

December 20: UN troops led by NATO occupy disputed areas including Vukovar.

1998   Croats allowed to return to Vukovar, but only during the day. Many Serb residents leave.

1999   Full integration occurs as Croats are allowed to move back to Vukovar; Croat schools reopen on September 1st.

2009   After years of rule by the conservative HDZ party, Vukovar elects its first SDP (Social Democratic Party) mayor.

2010   November 4: Historic visit by Serb president Boris Tadić to Vukovar and Ovčara, greeted by Croatian president Ivo Josipović, officials and representatives of survivors' organizations.

President BorisTadić: "I bow down before the victims to open the way for forgiveness and reconciliation…I come here to offer words of apology, to express regret, to create the possibility for Serbs and Croats, Serbia and Croatia to turn a new page in history. Everything that happened to Serbs and Croats in the 20th century can be put in the book of the past, which in itself would be an act of writing a book of the future…No crimes will go unpunished…We will finish this process of reconciliation and Serbia and Croatia will be two friendly, neighboring countries."

The two presidents also visit near-by Paulin Dvor, where 18 Serbs and one Hungarian were brutally tortured and executed by Croats in December 1991.

President Josipović: "A horrific crime was committed here and needs to be condemned. Revenge is not the solution….Crimes do not grow old. Croatia will always pursue the perpetrators of these crimes. This is our moral obligation as a state that respects the rule of law."

PREFACE

"Even today I don't understand why all this happened. I simply accept that it happened and that we all had a responsibility."

The stories in **Both Sides Now** remind us that wars don't end with the signing of peace agreements. The human tragedy continues to unfold for generations as children and grandchildren carry the legacy of their family's trauma. The task of healing a community scarred by neighbor-on-neighbor violence is all the more problematic; in addition to the human toll and physical destruction Vukovar lost the innocence of a society unconcerned with ethnic, religious or national identity. And that loss may be irrevocable.

Twenty years after the siege of Vukovar we are left with distinct narratives, and within each are multiple layers of personal stories and variations on what happened, of when and why it happened, and of who is a victim and who is a perpetrator.

Healing social wounds in the aftermath of war and betrayal requires breaking the silence, accepting the possibility of more than one "truth," and opening doors and hearts that have been closed to "the others."

Both Sides Now allows us access to personal experiences and opinions rarely, if ever, expressed in Vukovar. As one woman said, *"We work together, some of us even socialize, but there are so-called 'closed stories' related to the war that we never discuss."*

War happens to people one by one. These are some of their stories. They are ordinary people – young and old, women and men, professionals, workers, and students. They were not the decision-makers and were not necessarily heroes. They represent the thousands of citizens of Vukovar who survived the most horrific of all human calamities: war.

A Jewel on the Danube

Since 1991 Vukovar has been an iconic symbol of war and suffering, but the town has a long and rich history. Some 7000 years ago one of the first permanent settlements in Europe was located near the idyllic site of the town at the confluence of the Danube and Vuka rivers. Vukovar is strategically located in Eastern Slavonia – with Budapest to the north, Zagreb to the west, Sarajevo south, and Belgrade across the Danube to the east. For several hundred years the region marked the frontier between Central Europe and the Ottoman Empire. Vukovar was a multi-ethnic trade and cultural crossroads, considered to be one of the loveliest cities on the mighty Danube.

By the late 19th and early 20th centuries Vukovar was a tourist venue with holidaymakers attracted by the graceful Baroque architecture, Eltz Castle, the Grand Hotel (known as the Workers' Hall during Yugoslavia years), cafes, and fishing, swimming, and boating on the rivers. The giant footwear and rubber factory *Bato* was built in the 1930s in nearby Borovo with housing, schools and recreational facilities for the workers. Nationalized after World War II as *Borovo*, the company employed over 20,000 people from 23 different Central and Southeastern European nationalities and was one of the largest industries in Yugoslavia until the economic crisis of the 1980s.

From 1945 until its collapse, the Yugoslav vision encouraged multiculturalism and discouraged religious, ethnic, national differences. Although some tensions existed in rural villages, most Vukovar residents say ethnicity was not an issue in town: *"We never talked about those things before…I didn't think about who was what."* However, in the 1991 pre-war census 82.8% of the population of the municipality <u>did</u> identify themselves by nationality, only about 7% as Yugoslav, and the rest undeclared.

A War Foretold

Two decades after the destruction of Vukovar some residents now understand that the violence was fueled by outsiders –nationalists- and that the town was a pawn in a much larger game; others, as one person said, "*still live in the war zone.*"

Everyone had different experiences in the months leading up to August 1991. For some, especially in the surrounding villages, tensions were already apparent by late 1990. For others, life was normal until the summer of 1991 when an uneasy atmosphere of ugly words, threats and graffiti seemed to happen overnight. Suddenly it was 'us' and 'them,'… 'our people' and 'their people.'

This is how it can happen, as it did first in Vukovar, then all of Croatia and Bosnia and far-away Rwanda:

It starts with whispered rumors and blaring propaganda. Fear and suspicions begin to taint relationships. Neighbors become suspicious of one another, inter-ethnic friendships fade, mixed marriage families are forced to choose sides. Within a matter of days or weeks or months the social fabric of the community begins to unravel. Soon unsmiling people stop greeting each other in the market, on the streets. Uniforms and guns appear. Subtle language and cultural differences are emphasized and take on political importance. Shutters and doors are closed, children hustled inside. A person is no longer identified as a teacher, a plumber, or a mother, but by ethnicity.

Suddenly a diverse, tolerant community is shattered and deteriorates into open conflict. Suddenly everyone is forced to take sides or flee, to make life-changing decisions: Who am I, what do I do, do I stay or go?

In Vukovar by the summer of 1991 the neutrality of being "Yugoslav" was no longer an option. Parents sent their children away. The destination – east or west – determined by identity.

Centuries to Build, 84 Days to Destroy

If there are lessons to be learned from the tragedy that soon engulfed Bosnia and Croatia, the place to start would be Vukovar, where it should all have been brought to a screeching halt in August of 1991 with diplomatic and humanitarian intervention.

But two years after the fall of the Berlin Wall and just months after the Gulf War, Europe and the United States were reluctant to intervene in the "internal affairs" of Yugoslavia. The international community stood by and watched the total destruction of a town unparalleled on the continent since World War II. Thousands of civilians were trapped in cellars during 84 days of air and artillery bombardment that reduced the town to rubble, including the hospital and religious and cultural sites. The town's defenders, mostly untrained and poorly armed men staved off the attack and waited for help that never arrived.

On November 18th the town surrendered, in ruins. Thousands died, were wounded, captured, and imprisoned or executed at Ovčara. The battle was over but the larger Balkan war was just beginning. Vukovar had been the precursor for the ethnic, religious, nationalist nightmare soon to be unleashed.

The Aftermath

Vukovar became the symbol of the separatist aspirations of one side, and of the determination of the other side to deter separation at any cost.

Thousands of Vukovar families became refugees and could not return until reintegration in 1998; others stayed in the town and were joined by displaced families from Bosnia and Kosovo who occupied the homes of the refugees.

Vukovar and Eastern Slavonia became "Republica Srpska Krajina." During the years of occupation the town was isolated from the rest of the world. After Radio Vukovar went off the air on November 18, 1991, no news, no information about its fate was available. As one woman from nearby Vinkovci said, until 1998, *"We didn't know if anyone was even alive there."* Water and electricity were restored and schools reopened in 1992, but the town remained in limbo until the 1995 Erdut Agreement and the arrival of United Nations troops. Even then, little was known until reintegration in 1998.

The Dayton Agreement permitted refugees to visit in 1998, but only during the day. Finally in 1999 they were allowed to move back into the town. It was a time of great tension for both the "remainees" fearful of reprisals, and the "returnees," many of whom were survivors of the siege and had suffered personal losses, and all of whom carried the burdens of the refugee experience.

"No one is normal here…Ovdje niko nije normalan"
Graffiti in Vukovar

Many refugees never returned but instead were swept up into the great Balkan diaspora. Those who did move home faced a future of economic and emotional challenges. Eight years had passed since the siege but in that first dark winter of return the town was still in ruins, cloaked in the sorrow and detritus of war. Refugees found their homes destroyed or occupied by others, familiar landmarks gone, streets in disrepair and devoid of trees.

Accidental encounters with former neighbors, friends, or co-workers were fraught with emotions: betrayal, anger, grief or fear. An apology might be rejected, a former friend snubbed or turned away. For many, suspicion and distrust clouded any thought of reconciliation. Vukovar gradually repopulated, but as two separate communities, each with its own schools, radio stations, cafes ,and restaurants. The streets stayed dark and deserted after 5:00 with everyone inside behind locked doors. *"Before the war my parents socialized all the time,"* one girl said. *"They would visit friends and neighbors or have people to our house, but now they just stay at home alone every night."*

But as vicious and painful as the war had been, there were no acts of revenge. *"Vukovar is the most tolerant place on earth,"* one former soldier said. *"You would expect shootings and bombs going off but everyone is too preoccupied with survival."*

20 Years Later

Thirteen years after reintegration much of Vukovar has been rebuilt with the help of international cooperation including the library, schools and government buildings. Flower pots line new bridges across the Vuka. There are several new cafes and restaurants. A riverboat restaurant hosts an annual film festival and a ferry is available to carry passengers across the Danube to Serbia. Danube River cruise ships dock and tourists disembark for a brief tour. According to a local tour guide, most visitors don't even ask about the war; they are interested in visiting archaeological sites, in horseback riding, and visiting nearby wineries.

But for residents it sometimes seems the community moves one step forward and two steps back. A historic and promising event occurred in 2010 when leaders of the two formerly warring countries visited the town and a nearby village to acknowledge and apologize for the past; it was a moment when progress toward reconciliation seemed possible. But just months later events outside the community - investigations, arrests, and verdicts in war crimes trials — shattered the calm.

Life can be confusing and frightening for very small children from still-grieving families. One four-year old girl said that when she smiles, *"I only smile very small"…"because I don't want to make my mommy sad."*

Some young people share their parents' anger and prejudices against "the others" but many feel suffocated and are eager to escape the past and the town. *"We don't want to live in a museum,"* one young man said, *"the new generation thinks differently."*

Classrooms are still segregated but some students manage to rebel and break through the identity boundaries; they listen to music of "the others," meet after school or in clubs and develop inter-ethnic friendships and even romances, often hidden from their families. But for many the separation continues after high school when university-bound graduates decide to go east or west to study, based on their identity.

The community can never be as it was before. Over time a new Vukovar will emerge but for now the town remains frozen in its identity as the symbol of war and resistance. The shared interests and rituals that bind a normal community vanished in 1991 and have been replaced with memorials and commemorations that honor one side and alienate the other. Some religious and political leaders continue to encourage division. The policy of school segregation continues. Linguistic differences are emphasized as the once shared languages are "purified" to reflect the divergent cultures and historic memories.

Hundreds of people are still unaccounted for. For relatives of the disappeared, the war hasn't ended. *"We will always live with the pain until we find out what happened to them,"* one woman said, *"For us it is still 1991."*

Looking to the Future

Transcendental issues of facing the past, of justice, and accountability still haunt the lives of survivors. Should Vukovar be remembered as a symbol of nationalism or as a monument to the sorrow of war? Can there ever be a collective memory that lifts the burden of war rather than memorializing the suffering of one side? Can Vukovar acknowledge the past without becoming its prisoner? The human dilemma for survivors everywhere is how to remember the past and honor the victims without suffocating the next generation and the future of the community with endless sorrow.

Both Sides Now

Reconciliation is a painful, very personal, and for some, an impossible process. It requires empathy – the ability to walk in the shoes of "the other" even for a few moments. Our hope is that these stories will unlock some hearts and open discussion of the "closed stories" that are never broached.

The interpretation of history is most often left to the loudest voices. The silence of the majority leaves "the truth" to radical minorities. We have tried to present personal, quiet, mostly unheard stories. The narratives are often contradictory. It is not our objective to interpret or judge but simply to provide a voice.

We are grateful to everyone who agreed to open their hearts to us and to recount their painful experiences. Some of those interviewed have spoken publicly in the past, while others have never had the chance to tell their stories. At the request of many we have chosen to identify everyone only by initials.

The interviews were conducted in Vukovar and near-by villages during separate visits from 2006-2010 and were only possible with the help and support of my co-author, Sandra Marić and colleagues Željko Troha and Ivana McCue, and in the United States with my friend and editor, Laura Kelly.

Linda Garrett

INTRODUCTION

Someone said that memories are attempts for self-justification.

The first day we came to Vukovar in 1999 I felt as if I had landed in the 'place where god said goodnight.' You can't imagine what the town was like then. There were no lights, no shops, no people on the streets and just a few cars. Everything was destroyed. The bus station was full of poorly-clothed and ill-kempt refugees. I thought, what am I doing here?

I came to teach high school that September and taught classes in ethics, logic, sociology and philosophy at three different schools for six years. The classes were – and still are – segregated. The Serb teachers were all older and more experienced. Most of the Croat teachers like me were young people from Osijek and Vinkovci.

I don't know what we Croats were thinking when we arrived. We were so naive that we probably thought all Serbs had big beards and knives in their mouths!

We took the bus to town every day. We would arrive in Vukovar and wait in the only café, the so-called 'returnees restaurant' next to the bus station. We all felt very proud because we believed that we were doing something important for the city.

Our classes were in the primary school, the first school to be rebuilt. It opened on September 1st, 1999 with lots of fanfare, media, politicians, flags and banners. There were four classrooms in the primary school for high school students. This was a Croat-only school, with about 50 students that first year. I had to pay for all my own materials and books. When I went to the classroom the first day there were no chairs, no blackboard, and just one old table.

There *was* one place all the teachers mixed. Many Serbs were smuggling food and clothes and other things in from across the Danube and selling out of their homes. Sometimes we had sales in the school where it would be a typical Balkan atmosphere with a pot of coffee on the heater, lots of cigarettes, and Serb and Croat teachers altogether buying smuggled goods. Commerce trumped our suspicions and fears.

During the first year some of the students — the ones whose parents had jobs in the community -were very open and participated in the classes. The children of defenders always had the best mobile phones and better clothes and they arrived in new cars. The students who came from the villages were very poor and very quiet.

We never talked to the students about the war. I think every mother told her kids not to discuss war or politics. We were all very professional and didn't discuss anything controversial.

The first integrated teachers' meeting was at the end of that school year. The principal, a Croat, brought everyone together. I was late and sat down quietly in an empty seat next to one man. Then I saw that all the Croat teachers were together on the other side of the room. They motioned for me to come over but there weren't any seats. I was on the Serb side of the room!

I taught for six years. The classes were always segregated. These days there are more students, they all have chairs and there are new buildings.

Teachers in a post-conflict society are expected to teach new attitudes and values but their own identities have been shaped by their experiences during the conflict, so without professional support, they cannot meet the demands of the new society. We were invited to various trainings offered by non-governmental organizations (NGOs) but at that time we tried to keep our distance because in Croatia, and especially in Vukovar, cooperation with NGOs meant working against the government. It was very risky. So, really, we had no professional support.

An NGO in Zagreb recently did a survey about how much young people know about Vukovar, Forty-three percent said they didn't know a thing about Ovčara. On the anniversary this year, 2010, I tried to talk to my kids about it but they weren't interested. As for me, I forgot to put a candle in the window this year, and when I looked down the street I saw that no one had candles; before, everyone did. Despite the media and the TV, slowly but surely, the tragedy of Vukovar is in the past.

When I was a teenager in the 1960s we made jokes about the old Partisan movies and the actors. Now, almost 20 years after the siege of Vukovar the youth will make jokes about Serbs and Croats and the war. The new generation simply cannot comprehend what happened here.

There is still a lot of segregation in Vukovar but it isn't just between Serbs and Croats. There are also other layers of social standing between those who stayed and how long they stayed;

those who left and what they did; who was a fighter or just hiding in a cellar; who went to a concentration camp; who was abused; who had a relative killed…on and on. Segregation in the schools is just one of the many legacies of the war.

Although most of the houses have been rebuilt the inhabitants of Vukovar are more divided now than ever in history. They do not live with each other, but next to each other. This division negatively affects the normal development of the community. A community cannot truly rebuild if it has lost its spirit, its hope, and any sense of meaningful bonding.

In order to revive trust, develop a collective sense of community and build a society in which every individual is equally valuable, we must begin with the youngest members of the community. Unfortunately, in Vukovar the children have no possibility of socializing and learning together. This is especially difficult for children of mixed marriages or from other minority groups. They have to choose one of two sides and thus deny their unique identity. This situation just encourages social exclusion and social segregation.

The post-war divisions are expressed to the extent that children are separated into different shifts or use certain parts of the building, with separate entrances, and must choose which side of the hall to walk on, just so they will not meet the "others."

Today, almost 20 years after the war, the biggest challenge is to restore broken ties among people, to regain trust and respect.

Both Sides Now is an attempt to acknowledge and share the Vukovar war experience with those who lived that experience and with survivors of other conflicts. We also hope that the stories will be useful to a wider circle including scholars and practitioners active in diverse fields of reconciliation and peace building.

These personal stories symbolize human destiny in the town of Vukovar. The narrators have different backgrounds; they have different professions, ages, gender and ethnicities. They are ordinary people with diverse tastes and priorities. But what they have in common is their experience in violent conflict. They carry the same burdens, they share the same dreams, fears, aspirations, and hopes.

This publication represents a place for their voices to be heard through individual experiences, each colored by his or her attitudes and values. In preparing these stories we tackled the past knowing that we wouldn't all agree, yet with no discussion of who is right or what is true. The stories are in no deliberate order: they simply exist, one-by-one, each on its own.
Some people were willing to speak with us but others, even friends, colleagues, students refused, saying the past had nothing to do with them. They said: *"It is past, it is behind me. We*

have to think about the future," or, *"I don't know what happened in the war, and actually I don't want to know!"*

For those who did speak, the experience was often cathartic. We heard, "Thank you for asking me about this. No one ever asked me these questions. You should know the truth."

Sandra Marić

THE NEW GENERATION THINKS DIFFERENTLY
B.V. 2006

I was born in Vukovar in 1983, so I was eight years old when the war started. I don't have a lot of memories of the time under the siege. I do remember once when my brother and cousin and I were playing outside and saw a helicopter; my mom started yelling at us to come back to the basement.

We had a radio in the basement but it was boring. We just wanted to go outside and play. At first it was all very exciting as if we were in a movie, but then it just got boring.

It was dark, always dark in the basement. I could hear the bombs and missiles and couldn't sleep. I remember very clearly looking at the clock and it said 3 am. It always felt like 3 am. Once we heard a really loud whistling noise like a missile. It was so loud we thought it was going to hit us. My mother was so scared. This sound is hard to describe: it just gets louder and louder and when you're waiting it is very exciting. The missile actually hit a house about 300 meters from us.

Once we went to the kitchen to get some food and discovered a big hole from an artillery shell. I remember we said how lucky it was that no one was in the kitchen when it happened.

You had to know when you could go out to get food and water.

My mother cried a lot, but for a child, the war was boring. It was torture to be in the basement all the time. Once when my uncle's dog went out in the field and I was calling and calling him and wanted to go find him but my mother said no. I didn't understand.

I remember when we heard that Vukovar was going to fall. We left in October in our car through a cornfield and everyone was very tense. My mother kept saying, 'are you sure there are no mines?' You had to be clever and know when and how to leave. And you had to have luck. Some people didn't have luck or good information and they didn't make it. My uncle was some sort of officer in the defenders and he told us what route to take and when to go.

We went to relatives in Switzerland. My father stayed behind for a few weeks and I remember my mother calling and calling to find him and see if he was still alive. Finally he left Vukovar but then he had some problem with the police because they thought he was avoiding military service. After that he joined us and we stayed in Switzerland for four years.

The Swiss school was great, very different from our 'KGB' style of learning which was, 'just listen and shut up!' The Swiss style was more open, very participative. We were in a big circle, all learning together. Some guys didn't like refugees but it wasn't too bad. I learned German, French, English and Swiss-German.

We came back to Croatia in 1995 and lived in a refugee camp in Varasdin. The war was over but everything felt like 'death.' Then my parents got jobs in Vukovar and we moved to near-by Osijek and I had to start another school. It was hard to make friends. I was really heavy and unhappy and I got bad grades.

Then I became a Nazi, a skinhead. I finally felt that I belonged to something. I wore swastika symbols on my hands and arms. My father was always washing them off. Since then I have learned a lot about the Third Reich and Hitler, but then it just felt good to be in a group.

We moved back to Vukovar in 2001. Our house in Vukovar had been rebuilt by the government. I was 17 and again, another school. I went to Vukovar High School from 2001-2003. It was Croats in the morning, Serbs in the afternoon, then vice-versa the next week. It was very strange. There were a lot of fights. We had to be careful of the Serb guys.

I had failed my classes in Osijek but in Vukovar I graduated with the highest grades. It was better there; the teachers were not so hard on us because we were refugees. I finished high school in 2003 and did my six-month army service.

One month before joining the army I met a girl and we got together when I finished my service. She was a Serb and we met on the internet, at sparkle.com! She was my first girlfriend but it was a big problem for my parents and her parents. I was under pressure from my parents, but I said I loved her and they accepted it. They were worried though: What if she gets pregnant? What if we got married?

Her father was a supporter of Sesjl, and now his daughter shows up with a Croat! It was a big problem for a while. We couldn't go to her house or my house. But after a time it was okay.

Her father just ignored me, but I could speak normally with her mother. We were together for almost two years.

When we first met on the internet I knew she was Serb because of the way she wrote, and her spelling. I knew what could happen but I really wanted a girlfriend and sex! The first time we met we went to a Croat pub . She was talking so loud that I could feel that people were looking at us knowing she was Serb. I asked her to speak more quietly because I felt uncomfortable. She just laughed and said okay. We made an agreement not to talk about that stuff.

Later we went to both Serb and Croat pubs. It was never a problem with her Serb friends but a few of my friends didn't like it. Finally we broke up because things just changed or we changed, not because of our ethnicities.

My parents had Serb friends before the war. Now some of them pretend they don't know us and others just make small talk. One neighbor of ours is Serb and just pretends nothing happened, but it's impossible.

I have cousins in Sweden and want to go there to study. There are more opportunities and a better quality of life. The government here is corrupt and the society is intolerant and conservative. My parents listen when I talk about these things but they don't really understand. The new generation thinks differently.

THE PARENTS ARE LIVING IN THE PAST
R.K. 2007/2010

I was born in Vukovar but I was only about two years old during the war so I don't remember anything. Before the war my parents worked at the Borovo factory. My mother and I went to Serbia before the fighting started. Later my father came and brought us back to our home.

I went to primary school in Borovo Nasalje and now I am in high school. All my classes have always been segregated but the 1st through 5th grades were the most difficult The kids were at war. The Croat kids were always throwing stones at us. My parents told me to just be friendly and respect everyone. I really didn't understand what was going on.

The teachers didn't explain anything to us. Nobody said anything.

Things became more comfortable after 5th grade. I talked to one or two of them and then I went to workshops at the Europe House and had a nice time. I realized that there was something we had missed. I think all of us feel that way. Now we are friends. I think the kids who go to these workshops have a different view of the world

Some people still think the old way. They live in the past. Their parents are to blame. A friend of mine who is Serb has a Croat boyfriend. Her parents are okay with this but his father is not, he was a fighter.

Now all the high school students are in one building for the first time but in two separate shifts. We don't have any mixed classes but we meet in the halls and outside. Some of the kids still give us nasty looks. There were a lot of fights at first and graffiti appeared that said 'Send your Serb kids to Serbia, not to our school!' It was erased but nobody said anything.

I don't know what I am. I am Serb and I live in Croatia and I have to be okay with that. We just live with it and don't talk about it.

We have photos on the wall and Cyrillic writing in our classroom. Some Croats kids resent the fact that we have our own classroom. This school is not yet our home but we try to make it feel good.

I am sad about our town and our way of life. We try to be brave. It's really difficult sometimes like when we go to the sea. People can't understand why we still live here. We are just living our lives! The war is behind us. We have to fight for our rights. The Croat kids have better opportunities, especially the kids of veterans. They don't have to try in school. We always have to work harder.

2010

Now I am in my second year at the University of Osijek, studying Croatian language. I hope to teach grade school.

My father died two years ago. My mother and I live here in Vukovar. I hang out with my two best friends who are Croat girls. Last summer we went to the film festival together and did some other things. All my high school friends have separated, gone different ways. These two girls became my friends.

We joke about all that stuff. We respect each other in every way. One Sunday they came with me to the Orthodox Church and once we went to Novi Sad. That was the first time they had ever been to Serbia. We are thinking of creating a 'history school' in the downtown plaza where we would set up tables and all wear t-shirts saying 'I am Croat' or 'I am Serb' with the Serb t-shirts in Cyrillic. We would need permission from the police and to find a teacher willing to develop a real class about the war, to teach it without blame.

The schools are still separated from kindergarten on up. Nobody asks us what we want. You can either accept it or leave. I don't think integration is possible here because of politics and jobs, especially the Serb schools.

When I was 15 it would have been better to go to a Croat school but most of my friends went to the Serb school and I decided to study Serb language. Two friends who did go to the Croat high school said everyone knew who they were but they didn't have any problems.

A lot of Serb kids are paralyzed by the Serbian language. They are afraid to go to university here so they go to Serbia. My boyfriend is studying in Novi Sad. Half of my class is in Novi Sad and they will end up staying there for work. For me, I am paralyzed by the Croatian language; I'm from Croatia but I am Serb. My close friends know what I am and what if others find out, what can they do to me?

My Serb friends at university here are marked by the professors, everyone knows who they are. There aren't any Serb professors in my faculty but there are some in other disciplines such as science.

When I told my friends that I am Serb they said, 'so what?' One of them said she thought I was Serb because of some of the questions I asked but she didn't care.

I speak Croatian almost everywhere in town and at university but with my family and my Serb friends I speak Serbian.

My Serb friends are paralyzed. They know how to speak Croatian and they can speak it in public places like the market but they don't. It's because of their parents who don't respect this country.

HE PROMISED TO SEE US IN ZAGREB
I.G. 2010

I was born in Vukovar in 1980 and I have a brother four years younger. My mother was an accountant, my father was a truck driver.

When I was young I had Serb friends and Croat friends, there was no division among us. We didn't think about that at all until the referendum when people were asked, and then realized they were 'Croat' or 'Serb' or 'Hungarian' or whatever. They asked us one day in school and we went home and asked our parents, 'What am I?' My generation never thought about it at all.

After the referendum some things started happening. Serbs left some graffiti with the 'four S's' of the Orthodox church. Most of them were just adolescents.

Our best family friends were Serbs. When all the stupidity happened they stayed here but we all remained friends and we still keep in touch.

Most of our best friends from before are dead now. Many were killed at Ovčara including some Serbs. My personal closest friends did not stay here.

I was eleven years old in 1991. That summer we stayed in Vukovar until September when my father took me, my brother and two other kids and drove through the cornfields to Marinići, then to Vinkovci and Zagreb. We kids all stayed in Zagreb and my father returned to Vukovar. That was the last time I saw him.

He stayed in Mitnica and was an ambulance driver for the hospital. He was lightly wounded once with shrapnel when the ambulance was hit but he was treated and returned to the ambulance work.

We stayed with relatives near Zagreb. We were more worried than frightened. He called us once a week when he could but there were about 2000 people in the hospital and many wanted to use the phone, so it was difficult.

On October 31st he called and told us that our house was totally destroyed but he would rebuild it for us. He promised to see us in Zagreb. That was the last time I heard his voice. We had no further information about him until six years later, in 1997.

My mother stayed in Vukovar in the hospital with close family until October 28th. She left on the last humanitarian convoy with Doctors Without Borders. The convoy had some problems with the JNA; one truck was pulled off the road but hers made it out. After that convoy only the men could leave. Most of the children were already gone.

There were people in Vukovar who knew something had happened in Ovčara by the next morning. The Serbs who stayed knew what happened and knew who had been killed. It was revenge.

People were taken from the hospital to Ovčara but nobody from the Croat side knew about it except one man who survived. He escaped by jumping from a truck and running. After that he drifted around and was captured in Marinići a few days later. He was taken to a concentration camp in Serbia and released in a prisoner exchange. He didn't talk to anyone about what had happened until 1996.

Finally in 1996 he talked to the authorities. He knew the grave site. There had been many rumors. The government and the UN had tried to find the location and had dug some sites but until he got involved they couldn't locate it. I think now the Croatian government has him in witness protection as he is the only witness to the executions and the grave.

During the occupation we still had phone numbers of some of our friends and neighbors who stayed in Vukovar. We kept trying to call all through 1992, 1993, 1994 to ask for help to find our father.

In 1996 we first heard about the mass grave where over 200 people were executed but we still didn't know about my father. We had information from people who had escaped that prisoners were still being held in Serbia. We heard prisoners were in a work camp somewhere, in a mine.

Until the last moment we still believed my father was alive. Then in 1997 they called us to Zagreb to identify him. My mother and I went. I was 18 years old. He was identified by his dental records. They just showed us a photo, not the body. There weren't any clothes or objects to identify him.

Two hundred of the remains have been identified; 61 have not. Over 350 people from Vukovar are still missing; 1800 are still missing from all of Croatia.

I came to visit Vukovar for the first time after the war in 1998. Our house was in ruins. Everything looked so small to me because I left as a boy. All the houses were destroyed with only the foundations remaining. It was very quiet, very dark.

Despite everything that I saw it felt good to be back after seven years. I was running around like a lunatic on the streets where I used to play as a child. I was happy to be here despite everything that had happened. I came every two weeks to stay with my aunt. My mother and brother have visited but they stay in Zagreb and are not willing to move back.

I returned to live in Vukovar in 2004 after finishing high school and university in Zagreb. I studied traffic engineering but then had the opportunity to apply for a job here with a finance company where my mother had worked before. We haven't rebuilt our old house, but I think about it.

MY PARENTS NEVER SPOKE ABOUT ETHNICITY UNTIL MAY 1991
SB 2006/2010

I was born and raised in Vukovar. My parents never spoke about ethnicity until May 1991. Then one day my father said, 'If anything happens, you are Serb.' In Vukovar no one had ever paid attention to that so we didn't know what was going on.

Croats say the war started in May when the police were killed but for us the problems began in 1990 when World War II fascist symbols began to appear around the Serb areas and Serbs began to barricade the villages at night.

The brutality that began in early 1991 was initiated by criminals including one man I knew who was part of a gang that used to steal TVs and stuff like that. Then they started torturing Serbs and dumping bodies in the Danube. So the Serbs took revenge in 1991 and then the Croats took revenge in 1995. It was all about fear and manipulation and anger on both sides.

I was in school that day, May 2 when the police were killed, and it was chaos. The JNA came and both sides blamed each other for the violence.

Then my father moved back to his home village for work and when school was out for the summer I went to stay with relatives in a village near Belgrade until June 1992. You can't imagine what it was like to be in Belgrade and see Vukovar on TV, to see people I knew dead in the streets. My mother stayed in Vukovar, hiding in our basement during the bombing.

Most of the violence was perpetrated by the Serb reserves, the so-called 'Četniks.' These people were from the south of Serbia, from some forests somewhere. They looked like wild people with long beards and long hair and big hats. They were very backward, always drunk, and never bathed. They were the most brutal group in Vukovar from August to November 1991.

Some 'Četniks' came to my family home in November. They dragged everyone out of the basement and divided the Serbs and Croats. A neighbor in a JNA uniform arrived at that moment to look for his wife. He saw that something horrible was going to happen to these people and said, 'what are you doing, why are you doing this? These are our neighbors!' They threatened him and they killed three Croats right there, one woman and two men.

I returned to devastation. The Vukovar I had left a year before was gone forever. There were military and police checkpoints everywhere with four different armed groups roaming the streets: the JNA soldiers, local Serb militia, the 'Četniks' from Serbia, and Arkan with his professional paramilitary troops who were more disciplined but robbed banks and killed Serbs and Croats.

There was still no electricity or water in June but by September school reopened and I returned and graduated in 1994. My diploma is in Cyrillic and says I graduated during the Krajina, so even though our identity cards don't specify ethnicity it is obvious on my CV that I was a 'remainee' and that I am Serb.

After graduation my friends and I started a satellite 'University of Belgrade' hoping to avoid military service but I was conscripted into the Krajina army in February 1995 and served the last months of the war in western Bosnia and the Krajina. When Operation Storm started in August 1995 I was in command in Vukovar preparing to defend the city from the Croat army but we received orders not to fight.

Meanwhile thousands of Serbs were fleeing the Croatian offensive, some to Serbia and some to Vukovar. 'Arkan' and his paramilitary army were capturing Serb men at the border, shaving their heads, torturing them and using them as some kind of slaves. We tried to save as many as we could.

The Dayton Agreement was signed in January 1996 establishing the UN protection zone in eastern Slavonia. The UN troops arrived and soon dozens of NGOs also came. I started learning English and selling CDs to the UN soldiers. I was earning lots of money. I participated in the work of the Center 4 Peace, an NGO set up by Oxfam to promote human rights, democracy and inter-ethnic relations.

Then integration came in 1998 and it was very chaotic with refugees and displaced people coming and going. Croats started to return to Vukovar to reclaim their houses which had been occupied by Serbs. Some Serbs moved to Serbia. Obviously most of us who had remained here had been in the army. There was a lot of political manipulation trying to scare people into leaving.

The Croats who returned — our former neighbors — said, 'Oh, you stayed here?' There were a lot of rumors about who did what. Some innocent people went to jail. All my friends left and went abroad. There wasn't any direct violence, just psychological pressure. Lists went around with the names of people who had allegedly committed crimes. Even my father, who was away during the whole war, was accused of crimes; someone said they saw him with a big beard shooting people! And I received threatening phone calls. I see these people now. I know who they are. They won't look at me when I pass by, they just look down. I think they are ashamed.

Still today no one talks about what happened before the 'real' war started. Many Serbs were killed and disappeared between July and August of 1991.

In 2006 this is still a divided city, very uncomfortable. In Zagreb it is easier but here the situation is very serious. The local papers even have columns on how to speak 'real Croatian'! The "Nightlife" lists only Croatian cafes and clubs. There are two separate radio stations. It's ridiculous! During the 'Days of Remembrance' in November, Croats come from all over to 'celebrate.' What are they celebrating? I try to understand but I don't know what to think sometimes.

There are two words for 'potato': krumpir in Croatian and krompir in Serbian. So you have to be careful what word you use and where you use it. It's ridiculous. You have to measure everything and every step you take. Many leave because of this pressure..

According to a recent poll 60% of Croat youth listen to Serbian folk music. When a Serbian folksinger comes the Croat kids will go to listen but they won't tell their parents. An uncle of my wife was in the concentration camp in Sremska Mitrovica; he was tortured and abused. Now he won't let his sons listen to Serb music. One of them has a Serb girlfriend but he can't tell his father! No one talks about these things.

There are still many Serbs living in refugee camps in Serbia but most won't come back to Vukovar. There is nothing here for them. The government encouraged Croats to return but there is nothing here, no jobs, no future. Only old people and ex-soldiers with pensions can survive here.

But there are no pensions or benefits for Serb residents. My mother was wounded here during the siege, shot by a Croat sniper when she left her basement hiding place to look for water. She saw the man who shot her. He was a former neighbor! She still has problems because of the wound but she's not eligible for any kind of disability payment.

Now most of the villages around Vukovar are 'cleansed.' Most of the mixed marriage couples have left because it's just too difficult here. My wife and I are both Serb but moving to Serbia is not an option for us. Serb is my culture and my heritage but Serbia is not my country. It's a different society. I could never live there. So sometimes we talk about emigrating to Australia or Canada. It would be easier to explain things to our son if we left. How can we explain the stupidity of 'krompir' and 'krumpir?'

I could be a 'real Serb' and move to a Serb village and send him to a Serb school but I don't want that. I believe in some solution to all this, that is why I stay here. I gave my son a 'neutral' name, Luka, because that could be anything and because I always liked Luke in Star Wars!

2010

We decided to stay and are still here in Vukovar. Now my son goes to Croatian school. I visited the Serb school and the mixed school in Borovo Nasalje but I decided on the Croatian school. There aren't any Orthodox classes there but that is okay. I expected that he might have some problems but he's in second grade and there haven't been any incidents or discrimination. He is even the president of his class!

When he was five years old he had been offering some candy to a group of kids and one girl refused saying, 'Only Serbs eat those.' He came home and asked me, 'What are Serbs?' I was frozen! I turned to do the dishes and said we would talk in a few minutes. I told my wife, and then explained to him about our friend in London who is "English" and another friend from Zagreb who is 'Croatian' and that we are 'Serbian' in Croatia. He understood and said 'ok' and that was that.

One day some graffiti appeared at his school. The principal called a meeting of everyone: parents, teachers and administrators. The school reacted immediately and it was great. The mixed school is more divided and there are some problems, but they are covered up.

Young people here, especially Croats, are tired of all the war memories but the generation running the city came through the war. They try to pass the trauma on to the kids but the kids don't want it. They say 'Vukovar is one big graveyard! We don't want to live in a museum.'

IT WOULD BE BETTER FOR YOU TO LEAVE
SB 2007

My family came to Vukovar during World War II when the Italian fascists expelled all Croats from Istria. I was born here in 1968 and stayed throughout the siege.

I was studying at the University of Osijek during the months leading up to the war. Everyone knew something was going to happen after Croatia declared independence. We thought it might be an aggressive situation but couldn't have imagined what actually happened. No one believed that the JNA would take sides. My generation was bought up in the spirit of 'brotherhood and unity.' It was a turbulent time at the university. We are very close to the border and everyone was worried.

After May 2nd all classes were cancelled. I stayed in Vukovar with my parents and grandmother and continued to work at my part-time job during the summer. My younger brother was sent to Germany. We had telephone service during the first month of the siege but after that it was cut and my brother didn't know if we were dead or alive.

I don't think my Serb friends were aware what was going to happen but I do think a lot of Serbs knew. Some even warned us saying, 'it would be better for you to leave,' but we didn't take it seriously.

At the end of August the first tanks came to Vukovar and there were occasional bombings but still we all continued working. Even when things got serious, especially when the planes started bombing we still didn't believe the army would do what they did.

By September there was no running water, no electricity and the bombing was incessant, 24 hours a day even on days when a cease-fire had been agreed. We stayed in the cellar from then on, twelve of us including four children.

Our house was in a very dangerous location near the front lines, the neighborhood around the water tower. The enemy called this area 'the nest of the Ustaša' and eventually leveled everything. The planes targeted the roof lines, the tanks aimed at the first and second floors, and finally grenades were tossed in the cellars.

I learned a lot from the experience. What makes men and women so special is the innate strength we all have. Humor helps you cope. We used a lot of very dark humor and we found ways to entertain ourselves. One young cousin played the guitar so we heard lots of Spanish classical music. The children were age's six to 12. I taught them some English and we played a lot of cards. There was no electricity so we used oil lamps and made candles from lard.

The basement had three large rooms. We cooked beans, potatoes and cabbage on a gas stove and had a little smoked meat at the beginning. The defenders stopped by often and sometimes brought us a little rice or coffee or a couple cigarettes and we would give them food. Women in a nearby house baked bread and everyone shared what they had. Once in a while the guys would even bring an egg. That was the best!

There were snipers in the area because it was so close to the front line. We took turns going out to get water or potatoes or cabbage. It was a risk. You could hear the bullets whiz by your head. I wasn't afraid though. I don't know why. I think I didn't begin to feel the fear until later, when we were safe on Croatian territory.

We had to move to different rooms in the cellar depending on where the bombs were falling. We would always follow our dog and he would lead us to the safest part of the cellar. He was our hero! His name was Sverčo and he was just a little mutt. One day, he was hit by shrapnel and we couldn't save him.

Most of the defenders were civilians, fighting to save their own homes and families. They had great moral and psychological strength. They had few weapons and little ammunition but they were able to defend the town because they had the support of women and they were protecting their own homes.

Three days before the end we were forced to leave the cellar after a huge bomb hit the house. Thank God none of us were hurt. It happened in the morning and we immediately moved to a nearby nursing home with a large basement already full of people.

Finally our guys had to surrender so we could be released safely. They were thin and ragged and barely armed. We heard that one JNA officer berated his men saying, 'You couldn't defeat this miserable little group?' It had become harder and harder for them to continue the defense as more were killed. We were cut off at the end with no medicine, or food but they held off the third strongest army in Europe for three months!

On November 19th we were informed that an agreement had been reached and we could leave safely on the condition that the fighters surrendered. There was a ceasefire but still a lot of shooting as we came out of the cellar at about 2:00 in the afternoon. Everyone walked through the city and gathered on the south side, near the cemetery. Some old people couldn't be moved and were left in their homes and other refused to leave. Most of those people were killed by Arkan and his Tigers.

As we gathered near the cemetery we saw many friends, many people we didn't know were still alive, and so many children! One soldier was even surprised and said to me, 'We were told you were killing the children and baking them in ovens.'

So there we all were, guarded by Arkan's army and the JNA with a few UN observers. The guys surrendered their weapons and were taken to concentration camps in Serbia.

Then the second ordeal began. I really believe they were going to kill us. We were put into huge trucks and driven to Ovčara but there wasn't enough room there with all the people from the hospital. So the trucks moved to the Zagreb-Belgrade highway and the Serbs and Croats were separated. Arkan and his men went through the trucks asking everyone if they were Serb or Croat. Some courageous Serbs said they were Croat. One lady sitting next to us was a Serb who had survived World War II fighting with the Partisans. One of her sons was a high-ranking JNA officer and had arranged for her to be taken to safety but when they asked if she was Serb or Croat she answered, 'I was fighting with my people in World War II, Croatia is my country and I am going with my people to their destiny.' She stayed with us.

Finally everyone was separated and transferred to busses and we stayed there overnight. The next day the UN observers finally found us. Fortunately I was on the front bus because I was the only one who knew some English. I asked the UN people, 'Where are they taking us?' But they didn't know, they said they had been trying to find us and had been misinformed as to our whereabouts.

We were driven to Serbia while the UN tried to arrange a safe place in Croatia but apparently an agreement could not be reached. There were about 700 of us in the convoy.

Next was the most terrible thing for all of us. The busses were driven back through Vukovar. The town was on fire, there was smoke everywhere and we could see bodies lying in the streets. We passed one place which we found out later was where women were raped, tortured and killed.

From there we were taken to a farm in Serbia to spend the night, still on the busses. The next day we were driven to the camp at Sremska Mitrovica. A few hundred people from Vukovar were already there and we insisted everyone leave together. We said 'All of us go or none of us go!' The UN finally arranged more busses and all of us were driven from Serbia to Bosnia. There we were loaded into trucks again but this time, Croatian trucks and Croatian drivers! We were taken across the border and finally to Zagreb. The entire journey took four or five days

We were sure they were going to kill us but the UN was around and some British journalists were following us. They were our protection.

In Zagreb we were placed in hotels or with relatives. My family went to Germany to live with an aunt. I married a Croatian refugee and in 1994 received a scholarship to study in Canada. My husband died there of cancer in 1997, when our son was just one year old.

In spite of everything I now believe it was a good experience for us. No one in my family died. We learned a lot, we had friends who lost everything and everyone. I think my greatest accomplishment is that I was able to survive this without hate. I was more in a rage that Europe allowed this to happen.

My parents returned to visit Vukovar in 1997 but Croats weren't allowed to live in the city until 1999; during the transition the refugees were only permitted entry during the day. My son and I returned from Canada in 2001. He is happy here, it's safe, he can play in the streets, and he loves his grandparents.

But for me life is not easy. There are very few people from my generation here now; most of them were killed or live all over the world. It's hard for someone who is well-educated and has strong moral values to survive in this chaotic time. You are required to be on one side or the other. It's difficult to be an individual. I don't need to conform to a certain political agenda or be a member of a certain party to do my job right.

Survival here is an existential struggle. It will take some time for people to understand democracy, to actively participate and contribute, and to take responsibility for their own futures. We still operate with the mindset of communism, with the idea that the state should take care of us.

I am very grateful for Canadian hospitality. Canada provided a secure, honest shelter, a place to be and to be respected again. When you are a refugee it is a very undignified state of being. It doesn't matter who or what you were or are. But Canada allowed me to regain my dignity.

NOW THEY ASK, 'HOW ARE YOU?' NOT 'WHO ARE YOU?'
San.M. 2007/2010

I was born in Mačarska, near Split. My family had moved from Brčko, Bosnia to Mačarska 35 years ago for work. We are Muslim. At that time we were all Yugoslav. I have been Croatian all my life. I am Croatian. My parents respect the holidays but they do not pray or wear the head scarf. They are more open. In Mačarska everyone knew we were Muslim. There was discrimination but I was always the best at everything, to compensate. There weren't many Muslims in town but my parents never made any separations; I played with Croat kids.

My husband is from Vukovar and we met in Mačarska when he was a refugee.

I was only ten years old in 1991 and had blocked out everything about the war until I moved to Vukovar with my husband. I just remember a few things: a plane dropping bombs on the mountains; men in wheelchairs, and guns everywhere.

The most open kids were the refugees. I identified with them and we became friends because of the war, especially in 1992-93. The war in Bosnia was terrible for us; all of my family came from Bosnia as refugees. I was young and confused but by the time I was in high school I understood about discrimination

In 1992 my family was threatened but they didn't tell my sister and me because they didn't want to scare us. They sent us to Slovenia 'on vacation' after a woman threatened me. Some planes had flown overhead and a woman said to me, 'they won't attack us because they are yours.' She thought we were the enemy. I hated that woman but my mother said, 'be at peace with your neighbors.' My mother was religious in spirit; she talked to that woman and forgave her.

We returned when school started. I remember the sirens and running to the basement. I went to work when I was ten, we all worked selling fruits. Later I always looked for jobs. I was excellent in school but finding work was harder for us as Muslims. After 1996 it got easier Most of the Bosnian refugees moved away because the discrimination was too difficult.

I met my husband in high school. He left Vukovar in 1991 when he was ten, with his brother who was 17 or 18. They came to a small town near Mačarska. These were terrible times. His mother and father remained in Vukovar; she is Orthodox and he is Catholic. Somehow she made it to the coast to be with her children but things were very difficult for refugees. They barely had food or clothing.

My husband and his parents returned to Vukovar in 2003. His father has PTSD and both his parents are very closed. I moved here in 2005. I blocked out everything about the war until I moved here. I worked with a youth group and then as a tourist guide so I had to learn the history. At first I couldn't watch any films about the war but now I know more. I think it was my destiny to stay here.

I cannot imagine having children here, in these conditions with the schools the way they are. But I feel good here. I am a third party, which is a big relief for me, but Croats and Serbs continue to fight. I was a bit closer to Serbs at first but witnessed incredible nationalism. It's an age thing. The younger people are not so much into that. And it is better than before.

The churches are not doing much of anything. They just take care of their own. As a travel guide I take school children many places including the monasteries. It is amazing how we always hear 'we' from both sides… 'they have'…. 'we want.'

The teachers say most of the kids came back angry after the war. There are five-year-olds who say 'let's kill Serbs.' I led a workshop with Serb and Croat high school kids. I said 'let's talk about the war but if you want to talk hate you can leave.' They stayed and talked to each other, but only in small groups.

2010

Now I work as a professional tourist guide taking groups to Europe as well as leading tours in and around Vukovar. Some people come to see 'war Vukovar' but most are interested in other things like the wineries in Ilok, horseback riding, and old traditional houses. The cruise ships stop for an hour and I give talks about things like the river.

My personal life was hard the last few years but now it is better and I am very happy. The mayor is doing his best to please everyone and relationships in the community are better.

DIFFERENCES ARE AN ASSET NOT A DANGER
D.A. 2007

I have been living in Berak since I was married at 19. I am now 55 and have three children. I like to describe my profession as 'woman farmer' not 'housewife.'

I dare to say that my life was quite ordinary before the war. My daily activities included cooking, driving the tractor, gardening - nothing different from other women in the village.

For me the war started on September 2, 1991 when I was forced to leave the village. It was an evacuation organized by Croats. A man came to our yard and informed us that we had to leave for three days until the tanks passed. We thought we would only be gone three days but it turned out to be five years. One of our neighbors actually brought her crystal glasses, thinking she would return shortly.

All of the Croats were gathered together. We saw a sniper about 100 meters away. Nothing happened until we moved to the edge of the village and he shot one of the men right through the forehead.

There were three checkpoints. All the women and children were put on tractor wagons and taken to a small forest where busses were waiting for us. My son and I stayed in a village near Virovitica for two months.

My husband stayed behind to fight. One day they had to retreat and he was wounded. He was carrying his hunting rifle and the bullet hit the gunstock, saving his life. He was able to join us and we were together for the duration of the war.

Nobody ever expects war. Even when we were moved and taken to a neighboring village we thought Berak was different: 'It can't happen to us!' When the JNA came to the village in armored cars we all went out to see them because we were so amazed.

Nobody really understood what was happening at the time. There were armed men in the village at night. We had two cafes in town across the street from each other; one was Serb, one Croat and each began celebrating their national leaders of the past.

\

After the war I was the third Croat to return, in March 1998. Our house was large, in the center of the village and soldiers had been billeted there. From the outside it was undamaged but everything had been looted.

I'm not a fearful person. I was living alone in the house. I would stand by the window in the evening gazing out and thinking of how many people were missing and killed. In Berak alone 60 people were killed.

At that time it was a real adventure just to go outside in the village, to meet a Serb and greet him with a hello. I always had Serb friends before and I do today. But at the time of return two of my Serb neighbors came and said, 'you returned but you haven't yet said hello!' I replied, 'yeah, and you didn't say goodbye when I had to leave.' That ended any contact.

A month or so later my mother-in-law died. The custom is to keep the body in the house, then take it to the cemetery. She was very precious to me. I was grieving, very sad, but I didn't dare go to the funeral procession. I was afraid of the reaction of Croats because she was Serb.

Before the war the town was 30% Serb, 60% Croat and 10% others. The relations between Serbs and Croats were very special. We lived together and all worked for the benefit of the village. In my family for example, we had a few Serb friends we called 'home friends.' These are friends you invite to your house for coffee or dinner. We helped each other.

About half of the original residents returned after the war, but only a few young ones. We had four primary schools before but now there are only 12 students in the village.

The major problem here is not between ethnicities but between individuals.

YOU WEREN'T EVEN BORN THEN. HOW CAN YOU SAY THAT?
H.B. 2007

My mother's family is Bosnian, from Livno and my father's side is Ruthenian, from Carpathia. His people came to Vukovar 300 years ago. We are a people without a country. I only spoke Ruthenian until I was three or four years old.

My father was a music professor and my mother worked at the hospital.

I was born here in 1987. We lived in a house in Mitnica when I was born but then moved to our house next to the hospital. During the war we could see our house on TV because it was next to the hospital. It wasn't destroyed but some shells hit the roof.

In the summer of 1991 my grandmother told us that things weren't looking good. My sister was born on July 19th and we all left fifteen days later. My father stayed as a defender. We went to Germany for three months and stayed in a place near the airport but it was very traumatic because every time the planes went overhead I was so afraid I was screaming. So we went back to Zagreb and stayed in a place for refugees, a two-room flat with six people. It was very cold.

My father escaped. He arrived by the train in Zagreb with no documents and no winter clothes. He had been wounded in his foot and his head. It was very emotional for us.

He made a promise with the other men that they would not cut their hair until they could return to Vukovar. In 1998 they returned and all cut their hair together, right over there by the Vuka River. The media even came!

We returned to live in Vukovar in 2000, just before I started 7th grade. I remember there weren't any trees, the bridges with flowers were gone, and the city felt scary. There was one alley I had to walk through to go home; it was dark and I was always frightened.

I felt uncomfortable with Serb kids at first but later I was okay. Sometimes other kids would say how they hated Serbs and I would say, 'You weren't even born during the war, how can you say that? How can you tell who is Serb?' They would say, 'I can tell by their skin.'

In 2001 a friend of mine returned and we explored the city together. Everything was divided and it was very hard. The music school was the only place not segregated; there were more Serb kids than Croats but we all studied together. It was uncomfortable when I saw those kids in the street….Should I say 'ciao' or 'bok'? I didn't know so I'd just say 'aloha' or wave. I was a majorette and so was my Serb friend but we rarely spoke on the street

I think I was one of the first in my group to be open. I don't divide people by nationality. I divide by good or bad. I had losses in my family too. I couldn't see my aunt for a long time because she lives in Novi Sad. We could only meet in Hungary.

When I decided to volunteer here at the youth group my mother was in a bit of a panic. It was considered a Serb organization and she was afraid she could lose her job if I became a volunteer here. Some people said, 'Oh, so you are with Serbs.' Now, though, nobody talks about nationalities.

My fiancé was six years old during the siege. He was wounded when artillery hit his house and he had to be dug out of the rubble. His family returned to Vukovar in 1992 but he is Croat-Montenegrin so he had to say he was Serb until 1997.

The national media always comes here for the same story during elections. 'Are you Serb? Are you Croat?' Sometimes people are afraid to say what they are because people on the outside get the wrong idea.

My brother is in a mixed marriage and when he had a baby he refused to register the baby's nationality. He said, 'he can choose his own identity when he grows up.' Another friend from a mixed marriage refused to enroll his child in a segregated kindergarten, saying, 'he cannot go to school until it's mixed.'.

I WILL SEE YOU AGAIN WHEN WE ARE DANCING IN THE SQUARE
I.M. 2007

Before the war I was a truck driver. I worked in Germany for five years and saved enough money to buy a small truck, return home and start my own business.

The most important thing in my life was that I was a free man. I had control of my own life. And I had the ability to recognize that the state of Croatia was going to be established. I understood the situation. I knew I was needed and dedicated myself to that goal with all my being.

When I speak of my entire being I mean all my abilities and skills: intellectual, physical, everything one can possess to be dedicated to a goal. I took on the role of organizer of the defense of my village; of course I wasn't alone. I had a group of friends who thought the same way. And we did a good job compared to other villages in Croatia; none had similar defenses.

We prepared well. We moved all the disabled people and women and children out in August. Of 1113 residents, only 176 remained. A few of those were women and there were some old people who did not want to leave. Most of the people went to Istria, including my family.

We were also buying weapons, digging trenches, and in general preparing the defense of the village. We were very successful but in the end we shared the same fate as Vukovar: complete destruction on November 10, 1991.

Our idea was to fight to the end and then to escape, to break through the siege in small groups. The village was surrounded. At the beginning the siege was not so tight but later we were totally surrounded for forty days, which makes me think of Jesus's forty days in the desert. The town was razed and looted; totally destroyed.

While trying to break out of the siege I stepped on a mine and had 59 shrapnel wounds. I walked 1 ½ miles to reach Vinkovci. One of my friends lost his leg in the same incident. I tied it off and walked to get help. Of the six in our group we were the first to try that route; when the rest saw what happened to us they went across the bridge and were able to escape.

I had two operations. The first was in Vinkovci and then two days later I was taken to Zagreb and had another operation.

I managed to make a transformation. I think my path from truck driver to soldier and commander, to writer then artist and sculptor has been unique. I haven't met anyone else with a similar history. It must be the hand of fate. I never went to art school; my training was the school of life. I create art connected to my religion, to the sacrifice of Jesus and of all the victims. I have a sculpture of Ovčara made from a burned olive tree which, to me, represented all the suffering.

I will tell you the story of an old lady named Victoria. She was born in 1900, blind from birth. Her son left the village after the fall but she stayed. She was held for four months in a Serb village, then released and sent to Dalmatia to join her family. She had an operation there at age 92 and was able to see for the first time in her life! I visited her and said, "I'll see you again when we are dancing in the main square of B."

Unfortunately Victoria died at age 96 before we could return to B. Then, in 2000 I was speaking to an audience and told the story of Victoria who would have been 100 that year. The doctor who performed the operation was in the audience! Everyone cried. It was a miracle that she had gained her sight. Our whole village is a tragic tale and I am trying to safeguard the small stories.

I have always stood for the truth. We have nothing to be ashamed of here. I agree that war crimes should be punished but we committed none here. In fact, we protected three Serbs who stayed in the village.

We immediately knew who our enemies were: the JNA, the Serb Academy of Science, and the Orthodox Church- those who tried to conquer us - not the Serbian people who lived here. Three Serbs fought with us. One is now in Scandinavia, one lives in Pula, and the other died. His last wish was to be buried here in Slavonia.

Our monument to the dead lists all the dead with no ethnic separation.

PEOPLE HAVE TO KNOW THE TRUTH
FATHER G. 2010

I was born in Livno. I studied at the Faculty of Humanities in Zagreb, then Theology in Strasbourg, France. I was not in Vukovar during the war but have talked to many people about what happened here. I have been in the town since 2007.

I knew a lot about Vukovar before I came. I visited many times after the war, first in 1998. It was horrible. The church was a complete disaster. Two thousand shells fell on this church and, following seven years of occupation it was in ruins.

The Franciscans stayed here during the siege and were joined by two or three priests from Borovo. Altogether, six priests stayed in the basement for three months and were taken to concentration camps at Sremska Mitrovica, Staičevo, Belgrade and Niš. They were tortured and held there for about 1 ½ months before being released. One priest, Father Antunovač was held longer. An older priest in his 70s suffered a lot and died very soon after his release. Some nuns and a few other people also stayed in the basement.

After the integration the government eventually helped rebuild the church. It took years for the structure to dry out enough to rebuild and some people wanted to leave it as a symbol of the war. Finally in 2004 it was rebuilt and the priests returned.

Before the war about 45,000 people lived in Vukovar; now there are about 30,000 and of those, about 20,000 are Catholic. Most people didn't return.

I don't know why the Orthodox church supported the policies of Milosević. Sesejl and Milosević were talking about "Greater Serbia" and the church showed no opposition. In those years the Catholic bishops tried to make peace. The position of the Catholic Church is that the Serbs and the JNA attacked Croatia.

For Croatian families who suffered loss it is very hard to talk about 'reconciliation.' They have many problems. It is difficult for them to talk to a Serb. For example in Sotin, 45 civilians are still missing. The people have returned and they live with Serbs in the village but no one tells them what happened or where the missing are. These are hard questions. You have to search for the truth.

The youth don't go to school together. They have separate classes and this is very bad. Something is wrong here. There are many minorities including Serbs who opposed the war. Siniša Glavašević's colleague was Serb and he was killed.

Now and then you will see some graffiti from both sides.

There is no official communication between the Catholic and Orthodox churches here although we have some personal contact. In all other parts of Croatia there is an ecumenical week of prayer but not in Vukovar. In my opinion orders must come from some place higher for that to happen.

Would it be possible for the Catholic and Orthodox priests to appear together here in Vukovar? No, I don't think it is possible. It is not nice to say this but you can't go to a party with someone who has slandered you and pretend nothing happened. It's like a family argument: both people have to say they are sorry before they can talk.

People shouldn't forget what happened. They have to know the truth. Someone is responsible and must be prosecuted for what happened here.

YUGOSLAVIA IS UNDER ATTACK IN BOROVO SELO
R..M. 2006

I was born in Vukovar and lived in Borovo Selo. Before the war I worked at the Borovo factory and was an active sportswoman. I was also a tour guide and took groups to Czechoslovakia and Bulgaria.

People from 24 different nationalities worked in Borovo without any problems. But in 1990 when the right-wing Franjo Tudjman came we all began to realize there was a certain disconnect in relations between Serbs and Croats. Soon everthing deteriorated.

There is a book called "Crime Without Punishment" that documents the suffering of Serbs from 1990 until August 1991. Croats don't recognize this period as part of the history of the war because there were no civilian Croat victims; however, Serb stores and cafes were bombed.

Just before June 1991 one leader from Borovo Selo went to Belgrade to meet with Mr. Milosević and discuss ways to avoid war. He was kicked out of that office and killed two days later, possibly by Serb intelligence agents. His body was found in the Danube. He was trying to avoid war and civilian victims but that was not the Serbian policy.

During the war I was the commissioner for civilian protection in the Syrmium region. In May 1991 I was in the regional office in Borovo Selo.

The people in the villages had weapons by then. Sometimes they were distributed from the churches but mostly from houses, neighbor to neighbor.

On May 1, 1991 in Borovo Selo the Yugoslav flag was hanging at the entrance to the town. That afternoon two policemen from Osijek made a bet that they could steal the flag but when they arrived the local vigilantes shot and wounded them. That night the two policemen were taken across the Danube to Serbia. I don't know what happened to them.

The next morning I came to the police as usual, to answer the phones. I could see that something was happening, lots of people were around. The phone started ringing. Vinkovci and Osijek police called asking what happened to the officers. I said I didn't know. The police from Osijek said they were coming and then I realized something serious was happening because all the villages around Vukovar started calling, telling me they saw busloads of police approaching Borovo Selo.

I recall that it was exactly 12:03 when I phoned headquarters in Bobota. The man there told me they would send people to protect the civilians. I heard automatic weapons fire and dropped the phone.

My office was in the civic center where the shooting started. The busses arrived following a jeep and a car. They came right in front of my office, driving very fast. The jeep lost control and hit a concrete planter. A police officer who worked on the same shift gave me a phone number to call in Serbia and told me to cross the river and make the call with a code.

I escaped and crossed the Danube in a small boat and made the phone call. I don't know who I spoke with in Serbia. My orders were just to say, 'Yugoslavia is under attack at 12:00 in Borovo Selo' and to hang up. Then I took the boat back across the river.

Meanwhile the JNA from Osijek had sent tanks to Borovo Selo. The army ordered everyone to stop fighting and took control.

Twelve Croat police were killed in the village that day. From then on things escalated.

On November 19th, 1991 I had a group of 12 Croats working under my command in Vukovar and Borovo. Our task was to collect all the dead. We collected 1224 bodies from the streets and took them to the cemetery in Vukovar. For the first four days we had no instructions so we used big holes left by the bombs as graves. Then we received orders from the JNA and Dr. Stanković to take the bodies to the brick factory near Vukovar.

I had to walk two hours through mined cornfields to reach Borovo. Fighting was going on there as we were collecting bodies. I will never forget the horror I saw there. There were local Serbs and others who had returned to Borovo to rob deserted houses. They were just running over bodies without paying attention.

I kept a notebook with information about all the bodies, civilian and military. We couldn't tell them apart. Later during integration I was arrested by the Croat police. They took the notebook.

I don't have nightmares about that work, but I still cannot come down this road at night without seeing the bodies.

After that I was in Erdut until May 1,1995 when I was sent to Vukovar with the Ministry of Defense of the Republica Srpska Krajina to organize the evacuation of women and children across the Danube during Operation Lightning. We had protection by the UN.

I DON'T HAVE ANY NATIONALITY. SOMETIMES I'M SERB, SOMETIMES I'M CROAT
D.S. 2007

I was born in Borovo. My father is Croat, my mother Serb. I was just eight when the war started and I have a brother two years younger.

We stayed in Borovo during the war. My father had a hard time. Many people wanted to kill us because he is Croat but we had good neighbors with some influence who protected us. My father had always worked at the Borovo factory; he was fired during the war but later rehired during the Krajina government.

I went to primary school in Borovo then to the Vukovar High School after integration in 1998. It was Vukovar High School but segregated; ours was the Serb high school. All the schools were and still are segregated. Our first high school was in a building by the hospital. When we started there the windows were broken, the floors were in terrible shape and it was a mess. After two years the Serb school was moved to a primary school and then in 2006 to the regular Vukovar high school, but still with separate classes.

The first years were hard. Once in a while the Serb kids would have to go to the Croat high school for meetings. We didn't feel safe. Some of the Serb boys were beaten up by Croat boys during those years. Now it's better. A lot of young Serbs want to go to the Croat school because they have fewer classes and it's easier to get a job if you graduate from the Croat school.

I started working with a project called Europe House in 2002. We gave presentations at the schools and invited the kids to workshops with mixed groups. The first time we had about fifty kids, half Serb and half Croat. At the beginning they wouldn't even enter the same room. We talked and talked and convinced them to come in the room but they still wouldn't sit together. The next time only thirty kids came, and in the end we had a group of ten.

I'm working on a proposal with a Serb woman from across the river, from Bačka Palanka in Serbia. We want to connect young people to begin a dialogue not to 'make peace.' Most of the young people there have never been anywhere. We want to connect with them, to teach kids how to cooperate.

The churches have done nothing to help. I think they did a lot of bad things during the war. The biggest issue here is reconciliation and they don't do a thing.

I want to do something to make life better, to make peace.

I USED TO SAY WE WERE ALL YUGOSLAVS. NOW I THINK OF MYSELF AS A CITIZEN OF THE EARTH
S.M. 2007

I was born in Osijek and had cousins here in Vukovar. When everything happened in 1991 we went across the border to Serbia and moved two or three times while we were there. When we realized we couldn't fit in, we took refuge in Bosnia with grandparents. We were in a village near Knin then moved to Stanski Most.

My father had been a factory manager in Osijek in charge of a warehouse for tractor parts. One day early in 1991 some 200 or 300 people, Serb and Croat, came to the warehouse and told him to go home, that there was no more work for him after 30 years. When fear takes hold of people the loudest voice prevails.

We saw neighbors getting weapons in Osijek. We heard that Glavaš and his people were taking Serbs out of their homes at night and executing them. So one night we left, no headlights on, moving the car just a few feet at a time. We didn't take anything with us except I insisted on taking my comic books and my VCR. My brother, three years younger, was with us.

I was eleven years old then. I didn't understand what was happening. I had been beaten up in school in the 5th grade by older kids. I came home black and blue and asked my parents why this happened. They never told me anything. Once I even went to the Catholic Church! The priest kicked me out, saying 'you don't need to come here.'

In Stanski Most we were taken in as refugees and put in a neighborhood with Muslims. This was a beautiful experience for all of us. We were three refugee families surrounded by Muslims. We developed friendships; we had arrived with a lot of pain and found ourselves with these people of different nationality. We said, 'great!'

I was beaten up because I was a refugee, beaten up by Serb kids! So then I started to be friends with Muslims. I have a photo of three of us in school, me and my best friends – a Muslim and a Croat. We defended each other.

I started high school there in 1994. It was hard. We had no electricity or money for books or pencils. And I didn't like the school.

We had a small piece of land and raised some pigs. All the neighbors helped each other. We even made a little electricity with a bicycle wheel. It was a social gathering, a small light in the darkness of the war. Our house belonged to a Muslim family who had gone to Germany. We carefully stored all their things upstairs.

My father was always defending the families and he was against the war. He spoke out and was in a Serb jail for months. Then they put him in a non-combat job and he was away for two years.

I wanted to be able to protect myself and others so I took the examination to go to the police academy in Banja Luka when I was 15. The school was very hard; of the original 250 only 36 graduated after four years. Whenever I came back to Stanski Most on holidays I was wearing a uniform and nobody touched me after that.

In 1995 the Serbs lost that area and Muslims returned. My parents were refugees again, this time in Prijedor where there were 10,000 Serb refugees. I had been in police school in Banja Luka and left to search for my family; I finally found them. They were so thin it was terrible. That was really hard. They were living in an apartment with a Muslim woman who helped them. Always, it was people from other nationalities who helped us. My family lived on one loaf of bread a day.

Arkan and his people were there and they controlled everything from gas stations to bakeries. When I saw what was happening I went with two of my police friends to the bakery. We didn't have weapons, just our uniforms and we took bread and gave it to the people. We discovered that many men were hiding from Arkan and his people in the woods, so we took bread to them.

Then I heard about a huge warehouse full of food from the UN and U.S. Arkan and his people were selling the food that was supposed to be distributed to the people. I went there with a rifle and told the guards I would kill them all if they didn't give me the food for the people. They let me in but said 'don't make any noise about this. '

I was in the police school from 1994-98. I wanted to be a policeman in Vukovar. In 1998 I went there and spoke to the Serb political representatives to ask their support for my application but they told me it was better to go to Bosnia. The Croat police rejected me too. So I had nothing.

It was a huge disappointment for me. I had planned my whole life to be a policeman and it took six months to recover. I hung out with some Mafia gangs, played guitar, took drugs and drank. I had problems with Serbs because my accent is Croatian. I was threatened but I was tough. I made friends with kids from mixed marriages and then met some European NGO guys in 1999 and began to work with them helping old people, mostly grandmas living alone. That was my therapy.

It is hard here in Vukovar but there are beautiful people behind the clouds of politics.

EVERYONE HAS THEIR OWN TRUTH
A.B.. 2006

Someone should write about Vukovar and 'truth.' Everyone has their own truth and they believe their truth is the only one.

I have worked in Vukovar since integration but live in Vinkovci. It wasn't so bad there. I was a refugee for six months in a village near Brčko, Bosnia. My husband stayed in the basement of our house in Vinkovci and I took the children with me.

Everyone has good and bad memories of the war. For me, it was good to meet the village people who live a simple, calm life. My sister was a medic in the war, my brother was in the army but not wounded. Our house was not destroyed. Everyone has their own story and it's good to hear each one. The more you tell it, the easier it is.

In 1997 I attended workshops on non-violent conflict resolution in Austria, held by an American. This was before integration, when no one was talking. The UN took a group of us, Serb and Croat, intellectuals and professionals, to a place in Austria for seven days. There were 20 of us from Vukovar (Serb), Vinkovci (Croat), Osijek (Croat) and Beli Manastir (Serb). We were shocked to find ourselves all in one bus! No one said a word. It was very tense. We were all professionals: doctors, psychologists, lawyers, and people you would expect to be tolerant, but it was very uncomfortable.

We arrived in Austria and the leader mixed all the groups. We were never alone. We had to stay together from dawn to dusk; at night we had homework and then we sat together in mixed groups.

It's so hard to resolve problems. It was a step-by-step process: identity, superstitions, the conflict, and then role-playing. It was terrible. The leader created real situations like Croatian refugees: after 1991 that was a serious problem here when Serbs came and took Croat houses. Now in 1997-98 Croats were planning to return and wanted their houses back. We had to role-play the other side. It was very emotional. Many of us had suffered. One journalist from Vinkovci was very upset; he jumped up and said "I'll send tanks to kill you all!" But in the end, they had chosen stable people for this workshop; after seven days we returned on the bus and talked all together on the way back. We even sang songs from both sides.

When we returned we worked in mixed couples. We went out to the hospital, schools and other institutions and did role-playing. Sometimes the reactions were very angry; people would get up and leave. But 80% of the time it was successful.

Then we set up this institute, the first to be integrated. This was also the first project to bring children together to play.

Now we only work on conflict resolution and communication. People are forced to be together and communicate. We teach communication skills, better life skills, job and family counseling.

We were the first institute in Vukovar to deal with integration and there were lots of problems. Some people said, 'Oh, you are bringing Serbs here and making problems!' But we are proud of what we did! As time went on, many children and adults came through this place. We had Roma people too; it was bad for them before the war and still is.

I am an optimist; I know I don't always see everything that is going on. I think we need more. My colleagues and friends are mixed. Every time something happens now it's always about nationality, but the situation will stabilize. The youth are not interested in conflict and the older people will die. Everyone is beginning to understand that the important thing is how you live, not who you live with.

The institute made a mark. We did what we could to better society, to help families raise their children, and improve communication skills.

I DIDN'T TALK ABOUT THE WAR TO ANYBODY
R.St. 2007

When I was growing up I didn't know anything about ethnicities. Our friendships were mixed and I never had any problems.

I was always a pacifist, a rebel, and I hated uniforms so the military was hard for me. I did my military service in 1989-90. Most of the officers were Serbs and the soldiers were from all over the Balkans. I fought with everybody, spent time in the brig and finally a sympathetic psychiatrist helped me get a discharge.

I attended the University of Zagreb for a year and returned to Vinkovci in August 1991, just as the war was starting.

I think the Serbs here knew what was happening. A friend from one of the villages told me all of a sudden people were leaving their lights on at night, so one night he did too. The next morning he found a box of weapons had been thrown over his fence. By then, Croats were buying black market weapons from the former Russian republics. Everybody was preparing.

The Serb offensive against Vukovar began on August 24th with tanks and aerial bombing. The defense of the town was left to paramilitary groups. Everybody was a volunteer with something. I didn't join for any ideals, just to protect my town, my people, my family. I first fought with the HSP in September and October, defending villages near Vukovar.

My initiation to war was terrifying. I was with 22 other men in a house on the front line, near Vukovar when tanks blew up the building; 18 of the men were killed immediately. Five of us survived and were in the basement. I don't remember any sounds; I didn't hear anything. We managed to escape and I was really scared after that first fight. I didn't want to be alone.
All of us had to think about how to save ourselves. It was very dangerous in Vukovar and Vinkovci and we knew it would be safer to belong to something. Really, I thought the war wouldn't last long, maybe just a couple months and then I could continue my studies.

I left the HSP after that first fight and stayed with a group of defenders in Nuštar until May 1992. The first battles there in October were also frightening with attacks from tanks and heavy artillery. We were all so afraid, so inexperienced, and totally unorganized. I reached the point where I didn't know where to go or what to do. I couldn't find my friends and I just stayed there.

Finally a professional soldier arrived and organized the defense of Nuštar. After another big battle on October 9th I lost my fear. By that time Vukovar had been under siege for six weeks. Thousands of civilians were still there, struggling for survival in basements under constant bombardment. Some tried to escape. Almost every night we heard people coming through the cornfields saying, 'Don't shoot! We are families from Vukovar!' We were so sad about what was happening there.

Vukovar was surrounded and the defenders were running out of supplies. Commanders pleaded to Zagreb for help that never came but we managed to make several trips in and out from Nuštar. I went once. We drove through the cornfields at night along a path marked with pieces of paper to avoid the mines. It took us about four hours to drive through the fog. We delivered weapons and evacuated five or six wounded men that same night.

The only communication from Vukovar to the outside world was via Radio Vukovar. By November the path through the cornfield was cut and the isolation of the town was complete. We had listened to Radio Vukovar all the time but after November 18th there was only silence. The city surrendered.

I stayed in Nuštar but managed to visit my dying grandfather in Vinkovci several times. One day I asked him if he was ready to go. He said, 'I would love god to take me right now.' Just then an artillery shell hit the house and he jumped in the basement so fast! I laughed at him and said, 'Hey, it's just god calling you.'

The war was already taking a serious psychological toll on the fighters. No one was normal. Everyone was crazy. I saw people using drugs all the time: heroin, pills, opium – and these were people I never imagined would use drugs. We found enormous quantities of drugs in the Serb tanks and other places, and I knew some Croats who were smuggling drugs from Serbia to Croatia.

By the end of 1991 the Serbs controlled one-third of Croatia and I was high on war. I realized by then I was really addicted to the adrenalin of combat.

In May 1992 I was stationed in Vinkovci where we were cleaning weapons, building barracks and creating a professional army, but I couldn't just sit around. Many of us signed contracts as volunteers with the Bosnian Army, a semi-legal arrangement. I fought there during the rest of 1992 until 1994. The war there was crazy and I was crazy, emotionally out of control. During the big Croat operations in 1995, I was in Slavonia. My fighting days were over but I stayed on active duty until 1999.

Really by the end of 1993 I was having severe psychological problems. I was always in a bad mood, always angry. I couldn't communicate with civilians. I had all the signs of PTSD but it wasn't recognized then.

I didn't understand what was happening. I began to experiment with drugs, alcohol, pills. Neither my girlfriend nor my parents knew what was going on with me I didn't talk about the war to anybody. That was the problem. Even with my fellow soldiers; we spoke, but never about traumatic events. There was no professional help and no one in the army to talk to.

I always had to be on the move. There were at least five or six other guys around me who were the same. Of course the fear is there but once you start fighting you don't feel anything. Sometimes I would be shooting without any bullets! For ten or fifteen minutes! Then someone would tap me on my helmet and say, 'Come on, man, you need ammo!' During a fight you don't feel hot or cold or tired but after it stops you feel cold and start to shake.

In 1997 I attended school for mid-level officers thinking I would stay in the military as a career. There weren't any jobs and I couldn't concentrate on anything. Every time I thought about leaving the military someone would convince me to stay.

I was given sick leave in 1999 and got married. But the years until 2004 were my lost years. I received a salary but didn't work. I didn't do anything. I had too much time and no job. Most of my good friends had been killed in fighting or by 'friendly fire' incidents. A lot of the men were killed in those years because there were guns, drugs, alcohol everywhere. It was crazy.

I still have nightmares. My dreams are intense, full of people.

After war the main problem for every soldier is trying to return to civil society. Nobody understands. For a long time I couldn't be with anybody who wasn't in the war. None of us could live normal lives as civilians. We hung out together, talked about the war, and fought. .

Still today there are guys who just sit around in cafés all day filling out betting forms, drinking and fighting. Their pensions are too much, they don't have work and they don't have normal lives. If they are alone their lives are a disaster.

Most of the men in my platoon are still in the army or living on their pensions. Only a few have resigned and have jobs. Most of them are in bad shape, physically and mentally. I don't hang out with them much. There is that 'brotherhood' thing but when I see how some of them live, how they dress, I can't just hang out with them. I just don't like most of them.

At least 20% of them are in some kind of criminal activities. Four guys from my platoon are in jail for drugs, robberies, and that kind of crime.

Inter-ethnic relations are still tense, especially for former combatants. I don't like Serbs and they don't like me but I'm not going to act on that. I don't have any problem with them except I don't want to be friends. It's still too early for me. But I don't believe in segregation. I don't teach my children that Serbs are bad. It's up to them to decide those things for themselves. I think we have to educate our children for the future, to prevent this happening again.

When people ask me how things are in Vukovar I say that this is the most tolerant place on earth. You would expect shootings and bombs going off, but nothing like that happens here. I think everyone is just too preoccupied with survival.

FOR SOME PEOPLE THE WAR NEVER ENDED
T.D. 2007

I am the principal of a primary school in Borovo. I worked in a high school before but I find that the primary pupils are more tolerant than the older students. The younger kids hang out together. Whenever problems occur between kids people ask was it Serb-Croat? Usually it's not.

Our school is for all kids equally with no difference between nationalities or class. We want this to be another home for all the children. Probably about 90% of the students are Serb but we don't count who is what nationality.

The schools in Borovo were only closed for about six months during the war when all the children were evacuated to Serbia.

The children identify as their parents. As for me, I identify as a Croat citizen of Serb nationality. Croatia is my country but I can't be other than what I was born. Before the war everyone was Yugoslav whether they were Serb or Croat or Macedonian or whatever. Now Yugoslavia is shrinking. Because of the war there have been problems between Serb and Croat relations.

The former Yugoslavia was good for mixed marriages. Everyone was Yugoslav. Now there is no 'Yugoslav', so who am I now? If you are Yugoslav you are nobody! I lost my national identity. There were many mixed marriages in Vukovar and many people lost their national identity.

When you look for a job here they ask what nationality you are, not about your knowledge or skills. This is against the law now but it continues today. Actually, the most important problem here is unemployment, the second most serious problem is nationality.

Our curriculum is from the Ministry of Education and it is the same for Serb and Croat schools. Some classes are in the Serb language and others in the national language. For the Serb students, by law, 10% of the class time may be devoted to Serb studies.

The only problem we have with the curriculum is with some of the vocabulary in the history texts, such as "perpetrator" and "aggressor". It is not possible to have one history yet. There are many things we don't know and more time must pass. Every year the children are bombarded with a different history! It is very confusing for them.

During the first period after integration you could never read about Croat crimes. Now, 15 years later some things are coming out. It's not just black and white.

We have 323 students now but a lot of people are leaving because there are no jobs. Before the war this was a rich agricultural and industrial region but there is a diaspora of young people and those who stay have smaller families.

AFTER 19 YEARS I STILL DON'T HAVE ANY INFORMATION ON MY HUSBAND
M.P. 2006/2010

Five days before the siege started we sent our two daughters to Hungary. My husband, my mother-in-law and I stayed in Vukovar. At first we stayed in our cellar but on September 6th the house was hit by an artillery shell. We were saved by the thick walls but we moved to a neighbor's house. Seventeen of us stayed in the basement, including eleven children.

We survived without electricity or running water and very little food until early November but then the defenders had to retreat from the neighborhood and all the other civilians left with them. My husband and I were trapped there because his mother was very ill and couldn't be moved.

We were captured on November 8th, just the three of us. By then it had become very rough in the cellar. The enemy was so close and they were broadcasting Četnik songs, trying to frighten us into surrendering. On that day we heard voices upstairs and opened the cellar door to be confronted by a soldier aiming his gun at us, ready to shoot. Another soldier said, 'don't do that, can't you see they are surrendering!'

We were taken to a nearby school where we were searched. A Četnik took the bag with our family photo album. My purse and jewelry were confiscated. One soldier threatened to cut off my husband's fingers if he didn't tell them where the weapons were hidden but at that moment a man appeared who looked familiar to us. He ordered them not to touch us. One of the soldiers, a man who was later tried and convicted in the Belgrade case replied, 'Oh, and when did you become so sentimental and compassionate?' I still don't know who that man who saved us was but he must have been someone from our neighborhood.

He ordered the soldiers to move us to the Velepromet storage center that had become a concentration camp. When we arrived my husband was immediately taken for interrogation. He returned later and told me he was going to be sent to an army barracks for further questioning.

Then they called his name. He was taken away and since that moment nothing is known about what happened to him.

The next day I was moved to a camp in Serbia and then released in a prisoner exchange a month later. I went to Zagreb and started the search for my husband which I am still doing today.

The Red Cross had moved my mother-in-law to a nursing home in Serbia. It took a year before she was finally returned to Croatia despite all my efforts. She died six months later but never knew her son had been executed.

I know the man who took my husband out of the room that day. He still lives and works in Vukovar. I don't believe he was actually the one who killed my husband because he returned to the room a few minutes later but I am sure he knows who did. At one time I wanted to confront him but my daughter stopped me.

Croatian investigators have questioned this man and he has admitted taking my husband out of the room but he claims there were so many different groups of soldiers that he doesn't know who was responsible.

You can still see these perpetrators in Vukovar today. Many of them have been questioned but according to Croatian law, hard evidence is needed for prosecution. The government has promised not to close the investigations until the last missing person has been found.

Over 1800 indictments have been issued in Vukovar but most of those indicted have left Croatia, many to live in Serbia, northern Europe or the United States.

We know that some bodies were burned at the brick factory outside town and if that happened to my husband he will never be found. But if he was executed somewhere else I hope to find him. And hope never dies. Really, I just want to find his remains. I have an adequate pension and decent accommodations but I can never be compensated for his death and the pain in my soul.

We had Serb friends before the war but when the war started, we separated. I had one bad experience after the war. I saw a woman I had known for twenty years, we had worked together all those years. When I tried to say hello she responded that she didn't know me. After that I was so hurt that I didn't try to make any contacts again. I still see her on the street once in a while. But there are a few Serbs I meet and stop to talk to because I know they didn't take part in anything; some of them were also refugees.

Nearly 300 people from Vukovar are missing. Many people are still looking, mothers for their sons and husbands, children for their parents. Those who know the truth remain silent. We don't know why they won't tell us where the graves are. Maybe they are afraid of the consequences.

We started Vukovar Mothers in 1999. In 2005 we traveled back and forth to Belgrade to observe the trial of seventeen Serbs accused of participation in the Ovčara massacre. It was horrible to listen to those men who committed the crimes - to the lies and incredible stories they told to justify their actions. Some of them had been my neighbors! They were all Serb volunteers from Vukovar and Serbia. Fifteen of them were convicted in Belgrade in November 2005 in a very fair trial but the convictions were overturned a year later and the legal process continues.

2010

I met with President Boris Tadič of Serbia when he was here in November. Twelve of us from Osijek and Vukovar met him,. He listened to our stories. His eyes were full of tears. He promised to do everything in his power for us and we have some confidence in him. His deputy told us, 'just as in Croatia, some people have information but are afraid to talk, so it's hard to discover the truth.'

People who didn't lose anyone can continue their lives with no problem but the Vukovar Mothers will always live with that pain until we find out what happened. We continue to live in 1991. The most important thing for us is to find the remains of our loved ones.

FOR MY FAMILY SERBIA WAS A FOREIGN COUNTRY
N.S.2006

I was born in Borovo in 1970. I always had very good Croat friends when I was growing up there.

When the war started I went to Serbia, then was conscripted into the army and had three months training there. I wasn't happy about the army and never liked war. Fortunately I never had to do any fighting.

After integration the question for us was what to do? Could we stay in Borovo? I was born in Croatia, my father, grandfather and great-grandfather all were born in Croatia. My father wasn't a war criminal or anything so we wouldn't have that kind of problem.

Really, for us, for my family, Serbia is a foreign country. I didn't know anyone in Serbia. Where would we go? Lots of people we know went to Serbia. They called us 'bad Serbs' if we didn't go. One friend even said to me, "You are Croat if you stay here!"

At first there weren't any jobs for us. Everybody was watching everybody. Now it is different. Now they can see we are not like they heard during the war.

THE MARKET IS THE ONLY PLACE PEOPLE COME TOGETHER
R.S. 2007

I was born in a village near here and moved to Sotin in 1979. The town was majority Croat before the war with a very mixed population of Serbs, Hungarians, Germans, Russians and Ukrainians. It was very comfortable. I had more Serb friends than Croat friends.

But by 1991 there were tensions in the village. The HDZ had become very popular with Croats and the Serbs were suspicious. No one had guns until that summer.

One day at the end of August no Serbs showed up to work at the slaughterhouse where my husband and I worked. First the Serb children had disappeared, then the parents, and finally only very old Serbs were left in the village.

And no one said anything to us, not even our friends. One Serb girl thought I was Serb and told me to keep a light on at night because the JNA would come and leave guns for everyone who had a light. A few days later the factory manager told me that the Croats had ordered all women and children to leave for a safe place but the men had to remain. I took the children to Drenovci, then came back.

One day a Serb sniper shot at our house. We escaped, hid by the river for a few days then crossed to Serbia where we had Hungarian relatives. But after ten days my sister-in-law accused me of being a Croat Ustaša! She was having problems with her neighbors because of our presence. We heard it was quiet in Sotin and returned.

We could see the artillery firing into Vukovar but didn't know what was happening there. One day we sat on the roof and saw planes bombing Croat positions.

The Croat army came to Sotin for about ten days but when they left a group of us fled the village to escape Serb tanks. There were 17 of us. As we were fleeing, one Serb saved all of us. We were hiding in the cornfield and local Serb paramilitaries were looking for us, calling my husband's name. That night the good Serb came and gave us some apples and water and told us all to flee because we would be killed if we were captured.

We stayed eleven days on the river with no food or water. My youngest daughter cried and cried because she was hungry and it was cold. Finally we found a boat and crossed back to Serbia again. We stayed in several different places there but it was very difficult. My husband was arrested and beaten and died after he was released. He was just 39.

On November 20th Radio Vukovar called on all 'innocent' Croats to come back so we returned again to Sotin. There were two authorities in the village at that time, the JNA and the paramilitaries. I was ordered to report to the JNA three times a day. An old Serb friend came to visit and warned me to take down the paintings of the Virgin Mary. He said I should be careful and not go out at night or I could disappear.

We were threatened twice by the paramilitaries however the second time a young JNA officer came and he saved our lives. He took us across the Danube to his sister's house and from there we escaped in a bus to a Bosnian village, and finally arrived in Zagreb on December 27th.

I returned to Sotin in April 1998. My house was occupied by an old woman but she left after six days and we moved in. Only five Croats were here when I returned. The first day I went to the store and asked for bread but I used the Croat word for bread and the girl wouldn't serve me. She just stood there with her arms folded.

I don't communicate with my old Serb neighbors. I did talk with the Serb man who saved our lives but he has since died. The only friends I have now are also refugees. We are all old; the young people don't want to come back but I stay here because this is my home. I built this house. No one ever apologized for what happened to us. Some people said, 'Hi how are you?' but I just responded, 'Why didn't you ask me that in 1991?'

Two of my brothers died. One was a soldier on the Danube. Right after the war (November 19th, 1991) he was captured and forced to work with other Croats collecting dead bodies in Borovo. A few days later he died from a mine, they say, but his body was never found. My other brother was a prisoner in Sremska Mitrovica for nine months and died later in a car accident.

A friend of mine who fled Sotin with the very first bullet once said to me, 'Do you know how hard it was in Zagreb?' I replied, 'Yes, I can imagine how much you suffered when all the traffic lights were out.'

WE GOT OFF THE BUS AND WALKED TOWARD "OURS"
M.R. 2007

I was born in 1949 in Bapska and worked my whole life in the Borovo factory. I had a lot of Serb friends before the war but they were only friends during working hours, nothing deeper except for one good friend, George. When were all on the busses during the prisoner exchange I saw him outside yelling my name, saying 'all you Croats should be executed and thrown in the Danube.'

I kept a diary from May 2, 1991 until the surrender in November. It was confiscated by the Serbs but I remember everything and have recreated it day, by day, including the days in the concentration camps.

We knew the situation was bad after the events of May 2nd in Borovo Selo when many Serbs did not come to work. Barricades were going up in the villages and Croats and Serbs began to separate at the factory. Every day it was more and more tense.

I am married and have two children. My wife and children left Vukovar on August 4th with 35 busloads of families, about 2000 people altogether. My wife had family on a small island in the Adriatic and they stayed there until I was released in the final prisoner exchange. My apartment was destroyed by artillery on August 13th. My wife called a few days later and wanted to return but I told her no. The aerial attacks began on August 24th and by August 26th we didn't have electricity, water or phones.

On September 16th all men between the ages of 18 and 55 were drafted. I stayed as an unarmed guard in front of the shelter in Borovo Nasalje. On September 30th everyone was ordered to board trucks to Vukovar. There was shooting, artillery fire and we could see the town was already in ruins. Weapons were distributed but there weren't enough for everyone so I was sent back to the shelter in Borovo Nasalje.

I was able to phone my family on October 4th. I was exhausted. We couldn't sleep, we didn't have electricity or water and there was very little food. By November 11th the situation was so desperate that I even contemplated suicide but I looked at a photo of my family and just cried.

On November 19th it was all over. We ran to the shelter at the Borovo Komerc building and the scene was horrific. The basement was full of about 700 women and children and old people, all in despair. When they saw us they cried, kissed and hugged us.

We were captured outside the building by JNA and Četniks. They searched us and sent us to a hangar then put everyone on busses first to Sremska Mitrovica and then on to Staičevo, a cattle farm, where we were herded into a stable to sleep on concrete floors. About 1300 or 1500 of us were held there for 35 days. We were beaten and tortured mentally and physically. The guards were JNA reserves, you could say 'Četniks' with military police uniforms.

The first ten days were terrible. It was -20 degrees centigrade. We sat and slept on the concrete with just one thin blanket. Finally on November 31st the Red Cross arrived and made a list of everyone and we were given hay to sleep on. But we were still constantly provoked, kicked, hit beaten.

On December 22nd we were moved to a camp at Niš. Here the guards were regular JNA army, just young kids really. However, every time we arrived at a new location they were told 'the Ustaša are coming' so we received 'special welcomes.' They would line up and beat us with bats, hands, fists and boots. But after 35 days sleeping on concrete we finally had beds with sheets and blankets. On January 15th all hell broke loose. We were beaten, kicked and stomped on. We didn't know why until the next day we found out that Croatian independence had been recognized.

Prisoner exchanges came and went but I was never included. On February 15th we were moved again, to Sremska Mitrovica. More prisoner exchanges, more abuse. By August I had lost ten kilos and my hair had turned grey. Finally, on August 14th, 1992 we were taken on busses to a place near Nemetin. At 4:15 pm the busses stopped and we saw Croat busses. We got off walked toward "ours." Our people were waiting for us, reaching out their hands in welcome. I cried and hugged everyone. We drove to Osijek where a huge crowd of people welcomed us. After 270 days we were free. I was reunited with my wife on August 15th. We went to Germany for 16 months and then stayed in a hotel in Gurđevac from 1994 until 1999. I still suffer from neck and spinal problems and pain from the beatings on the bottom of my feet.

After all the struggle to return to Vukovar I also had to fight a battle in court for my apartment because it was occupied by a Serb. Finally in 1999 we were able to return to live in our home.

ALL MOTHERS SHED THE SAME TEARS
Father J. 2007

I was born in Vukovar in 1974 but always lived in Borovo Village. I studied for the priesthood in Serbia from 1988 to 1993, then returned here to work.

My dad was a painter in Vukovar and my mom worked in the Borovo factory. My parents divorced when I was young and I stayed with my father.

When I came back home to visit in 1990 it looked like a movie! There were posters of Tudjman and Croat flags and symbols everywhere. Then the next year we saw shooting on TV and I knew something was happening.

When the war started my dad told me not to come. We didn't have any contact until July 1991 when we met in Serbia. My brother and grandmother and the mother of my stepmother were all there - refugees from Vukovar - and I went to see them.

Then toward the middle of November I secretly visited our house in Vukovar. It was a very difficult journey from Serbia. There was shooting everywhere. I crossed the Danube on a boat and the soldiers told me, 'you're on your own.' There were artillery shells and grenades exploding everywhere. The sky was very dark. I didn't think about the danger because I wanted to see my father so badly.

I walked from the river to our house. There was no water or electricity but the house was undamaged. I sat with my grandmother for two days listening to the BOOMs. It was a catastrophe. It was extremely cold but we had a wood fire.

After two days my father came home and he was so angry when he saw me! The next day I went back to Serbia as I only had a three-day leave from classes. I crossed the river on about November 15th. I had come at the very worst time.

I returned again in December 1991. I remember walking through the town. The church and all the buildings were totally destroyed. A priest told me he had seen the church perimeter mined.

I ask myself all the time why the war happened. I could never have imagined what possible reasons there could be for war. The Croatian government was wrong in its policies. All of us who lived in Croatia had Croatian stamps on our documents and it was the same in Serbia. Why did they have to become nationalistic? It was totally wrong. I feel very sad about everyone who died in the war, and in the end, the Croatian government didn't get what it wanted: to ethnically cleanse the region. Serbs are still here. They came hundreds of years ago. The proof is that monasteries have been here for centuries.

The main Orthodox Church in Vukovar was built in 1737, the Catholic Church in 1874. Many Serbs moved here after the Battle of Kosovo in 1389. The point of this is that there was no justification for war.

I don't care about borders. Everyone should respect the country they are in. Serbia is wherever I set my foot because I am Serbian.

After all these years why did the war happen? We had a beautiful life. I think about this all the time but will never understand. I could never hate enough to kill. I lost my youth because of the war.

Integration was a horror. During the days prior, in December 1997, the home of the priests was bombed on the day of the Catholic Christmas. The house was damaged but luckily no one was injured.

In January 1998 the people were afraid because of what happened during Operation Storm. Everyone panicked. What will happen to us? We kept telling people to stay but many left. The United Nations was little help. I was in many meetings with them but they closed their eyes to what was going on and did not respond. At that time many Serbs went to Australia, Canada, England, Norway and Ireland. No one comes back here.

Now, again there are tensions. They are constantly talking about war crimes, insisting on that story! We are all Christians and we should all confess; once you confess there is one less sinner. I say everyone should clean his own house.

For me, it is impossible that one person should kill another. But unfortunately there were victims and they are still being manipulated. It is not true that no Serbs were killed; many were killed in Operations Storm and Lightning. The very first victim in Vukovar was a Serb man who was killed in front of his house.

Our Patriarch once said, 'We have to forgive but we mustn't forget.' This must be our lesson. We should all work on ourselves, to build a better future. We can't change the past. I say with respect, all mothers shed the same tears.

Young Serbs are comfortable here. Me, too. This is my country. No one has more rights than I do. The name of the country doesn't matter; it was Austria-Hungary before, now it's Croatia and later it could be something else.

Jobs are the most important thing for everyone. When a person is busy he doesn't have time to think about stupid things, just to plan a better future for his family. The lack of jobs is the main reason for problems here. There are still people searching through the trash for food! If you have a job, a work schedule and you don't sit in front of the TV all day listening to politicians you are worth something, you are productive.

I truly believe people will change. Love will prevail. Love was missing here and that is why it happened. Vukovar will change. Soon the war will be 20 years in the past.

MANY PEOPLE THOUGHT VUKOVAR HAD BEEN BETRAYED
S.J. 2007

I was born in Bosnia-Herzegovina in 1965. I am Croat and I came to Vukovar in 1985 because I fell in love – first with the woman who was to be my wife, and then with Vukovar.

I had attended primary school and the first two years of high school in Bosnia. When I arrived in Vukovar I worked in agriculture, construction, and odd jobs and then finished secondary school in Belgrade. I returned to Vukovar, worked as a butcher and had a daughter in 1987. We always lived in the Sajmište neighborhood of Vukovar.

When the police were killed in Borovo Selo on May 2nd we all felt something deep inside. I quit my job the next day and joined the forces being organized by HDZ. At the beginning most of the people had some kind of weapons but others like me didn't have any guns or money so we just had to wait.

From May until August 24th we were organizing ourselves in Sajmište near the Vuteks building. We sandbagged some buildings and began a night watch. The JNA base was near us so we watched their activities. During the day they would drive to a warehouse near Brsadin, load up a truck with weapons and supplies and distribute them to the Serb population at night. Serbs were told to use white paint to make a sign, a cross on their houses.

There were a few incidents during that period, usually provoked by Serbs. They would drive around, usually drunk, with weapons in the car provoking people. These were all local Serbs, people we knew. The Serbs who came from Serbia usually stayed in the villages.

Our only mission was to watch and keep notes. Nothing serious happened before August 24th, just sporadic shooting. On that day the tanks came from Negoslavci, then turned off at

Vučedol because of the mines. We really didn't think this was going to be WAR. We weren't expecting anything serious.

There were just a few guys in the JNA camp in town. When they tried to escape in a tank we destroyed it and another military vehicle so they couldn't leave. But we had strict orders from Zagreb not to fight with them.

We had four battalions: Sajmište was the First Battalion, Mitnica the Second, Borovo Selo the Third, and Grad was the Fourth Battalion. In Sajmište we had about 450 guys but our area was different from Borovo and Mitnica. Those areas had straight front lines but our neighborhood had more Serbs than Croats so there was street-to-street fighting everywhere.

On September 13th the Serbs launched the first serious attack on Sajmište. We fought them off. They tried the next day, again with tanks and infantry and again we stopped them. On September 15th they took part of the neighborhood.

I was wounded on September 28th. We had been on night watch near Vuteks and in the morning we had to clean out the area. Some Serbs who had managed to hide in the attic of a house during the night threw grenades and tear gas and I was hit. The medics came and we drove to the hospital. Snipers were firing at us and shrapnel from an artillery attack hit the vehicle. I had shrapnel wounds in my leg and neck and the shrapnel is still in my body.

The hospital was crazy at that time. The seriously wounded were in the basement, lightly wounded on the upper floor and operations took place where the museum is now. My operation was in a corridor, with no anesthesia.

I left after three days and spent the rest of the siege in Sajmište, Olajnića and in the neighborhood around the train tracks by the Vuka River. On the night of November 17th-18th we took a chance to escape toward Nuštar. The area had been mined by Croats; the guy who did the mining led the groups out. When he took us through the minefield he went back again and then disappeared; no one knows what happened to him. He was never found or captured.

We crossed the Vuka in a small children's boat. During the daylight hours we stayed hidden in the bushes and then traveled at night. We went around Nuštar and took the road to Vinkovci. In one Serb house we found a huge kulen. We took it and I said, 'I swear to god I am going to eat this in Zagreb!'

The entire trip took two nights and three days, often passing under the noses of the Serbs. We went to a hotel in Vinkovci, then took a bus to Zagreb the next day. We forced the driver to go right through the center of Zagreb, down a pedestrian-only street because we were so pissed off to see everything looking completely normal. We wanted to destroy the big monument in the center of the city but we just put a Croatian flag on it and then prayed. People came up and asked us who we were and where we were from!

The next day in the hotel we asked for some bread and shared the kulen and a couple drinks.

Out of the 100 in our group, 38 escaped. About 200-300 defenders made it out . In December I joined the HOS and fought in Croatia and Bosnia. I returned to Vukovar at Christmas time in 1998 and received my pension. Now I am the coordinator of the veterans' groups, concentration camp survivors, and the disabled.

I DON'T WANT TO HAVE TO SAY WHAT I AM
I.P.M. 2010

I was born in Vukovar to a mixed family, mostly Czech but I am everything: Czech, Croat, Serb, Hungarian, Jewish! It never mattered before the war.

My father was a lawyer and the director of the port and my mother was a teacher. My family lived in Vukovar for hundreds of years and we have had generations of lawyers.

I was 15 in 1991. The last year before the war we suddenly knew who was what. I was in the middle! I didn't know anything. I remember some girls arguing about Serb and Croat, and then some Serb businesses were destroyed.

In the summer of 1991 my mother took me and some other kids to Hvar where we had a house. At the end of August we went to Sarajevo and then tried to return to Vukovar but all the roads were closed. We had these other kids with us but didn't know how to find their parents. So we drove to Novi Sad to stay with family and I went to school there that year, 1991-92.

We returned to Vukovar in the summer of 1992. I couldn't recognize anything. There weren't any streets. There were soldiers everywhere. Our house was destroyed. I moved in with my boyfriend whose family had a huge villa with a swimming pool but all the windows in the house had been broken, so there were no windows.

Classes were resumed in Vukovar in September of 1992 so I finished my last year of secondary school. There were many refugee kids from Osijek, Zadar, all over the country. We were confused and crazy then. We were teenagers! We just walked around, even at night.

I remember one New Year's Eve. We went to a party all dressed up with high heels and make-up. When we returned home at midnight, machine guns were firing everywhere. We had to lie down in the street with our heels and make-up and bullets flying all around us!

I finished high school in 1993 and stayed nine years in Vukovar with my boyfriend. But you had to be connected to get a job. I remember one interview where they said, 'You're not a Serb. You'll never get a job here.'

In 1997 I left my boyfriend and Vukovar and went to Tenerife to work. At that time the tension here was terrible because everyone was afraid about the integration to come in 1998. There were stories and rumors everywhere, people were saying 'we'll lose our jobs, our houses, we'll have to leave.' I couldn't function. I had PTSD. I knew there would be a lot of conflict and problems and I was right: 1998 was the worst year for many people. No one knew what to think after so many years of separation.

The situation is better now. I returned to Vukovar in 2007 and I am taking law classes. There were generations of lawyers in our family but now there are no boys so they expect me to be the lawyer!

Even now I have to choose but I don't want to. I don't want to say what I am. There is nothing on my birth certificate because my parents refused to answer the question when I was born.

My daughter is ten. She was born in Spain and her father is Scottish. I put her in the Croat school. At school they talk about the war a lot. Some of the kids say Serbs are devils. At first my daughter was afraid to say she is part Serb but now she tells me, 'Mom half my class is Serb!' Every year there are fewer kids in the Serb schools but they will never close because integration would mean a loss of jobs.

WE HAVE ALWAYS BEHAVED AS YUGOSLAVS
S.V. 2006/2010

I was born in Vukovar, the only child in a mixed marriage. I considered myself a Yugoslav, but at the time of separation, I was forced to choose. Since the custom here is that origin is determined by the father, I became Serb.

I graduated from Vukovar High School, then the University of Osijek with a degree in Croatian-Serbian Language and Literature but the only work I could find in Vukovar was clerking in a grocery store and that is where I was when war broke out in August 1991.

When the war started I thought about who my friends were and to my surprise I realized that of all of them, only two were Serb. I had never thought about it before.

I was completely apolitical but I could see the beginnings of conflict even in 1990 with the resurgence of nationalism. That year a Croat friend said, 'At last we'll be given the opportunity for jobs after all the Serbs have been kicked out.' I was shocked and said, 'then I will be forced to leave!' She said, 'No, you are our Serb.'

I could see the situation was becoming serious early in 1991 when some of my former classmates joined the ZNG and began wearing uniforms and carrying Kalashnikovs. A few of them even stopped greeting me in the streets. My boyfriend was Croat. He also joined and tried to convince me that an independent Croatia would be like Switzerland. I was afraid. We started to have arguments and to grow apart. Later he was very active in the defense of Vukovar and was wounded.

We always lived in Šajmište. It was a mixed neighborhood and the fighting was very intense from August 24th until it was taken by the JNA and Serb paramilitary. We stayed in our basement for eight weeks. One end of my street was close to the Serb line and the Croat army was at the other end. We were constantly bombarded day and night. Finally our neighborhood was taken by Serbs at the end of October.

Then we were able to go out and look for supplies. We were low on everything. For the first time in my life I hadn't eaten for three days. I was the youngest person in the basement so I was sent out to look for medication for one man who was diabetic and needed help. A neighbor told me that if I drove very fast I could make it to the village that was headquarters for the JNA, ten kilometers to the south.

I drove the diabetic man to the village and stayed with relatives. I was so surprised to see they had an abundance of food: meat, cookies, cakes! In Vukovar we lived in hell and just ten kilometers away they were living in heaven. I took my first shower in weeks and rested.

The diabetic man decided he would go to Belgrade for medical treatment and asked me to accompany him. The only way to travel was via military transport so three days later we left in a truck carrying wounded men back to Belgrade. This journey was terrible. A young man was lying on the floor of the truck next to me, seriously wounded and bleeding heavily. My hand was in that blood. He was very young and cried out, 'mother, my dear mother.' It felt as though that journey lasted years.

I stayed with my aunt in Belgrade for a month but couldn't communicate with my parents so I returned to Vukovar at the end of November. The town was destroyed and nearly abandoned but my parents and our home had survived.

I had intended to stay for just a few days and immediately travel back to Belgrade. I applied for a travel permit from the JNA but was ordered to stay because I was needed to start a radio station. I was confused. I didn't know anything about radio or journalism! I didn't know where to begin. I was taken to a large house that had been abandoned by a Croat family and told that it would be the home of the radio station.

Several people were assigned to work with me. The furnishings included a bed, a chair and an old radio mixer. For the next two or three years we were paid in the form of food and other supplies.

The radio was intended to be a news and information service for the estimated 2,000 – 5,000 civilians remaining in Vukovar. The first broadcast was December 4th, 1991 at 2:00 pm. I was the editor-in-chief and wrote the text for the first program, explaining that this was the new Radio Dunav, the voice of the Serb government of Krajina.

Everyone was enthusiastic and no one interfered with our programs. We broadcast just two hours a day with lots of nationalistic Serb music to lift spirits. We told people where to find supplies, what streets were safe, where mines were located and so on.

Vukovar was grey: the sky, the houses, and the people. It was cold. There was rubble everywhere: bricks, cement, roof tiles, window frames. It was a complete mess. It was wet and raining and everything turned to mud, increasing the impression of grey. It was always foggy, people moved around with boots on. You rarely saw civilians in the streets, only military personnel, and so that, together with the ruined buildings, made Vukovar look like a ghost town.

The electricity didn't come back on until June 1992 and there was no running water until the next autumn. You can imagine what it was like for me, a spoiled only child writing reports by gas lamp and washing myself with just a little pot of hot water!

There wasn't any fighting here after November, just defensive positions. We were under martial law and completely isolated. The city was 75% destroyed. The refugees in Serbia started to return and the process of cleaning up was organized.

It was dangerous, however. There were lots of paramilitaries. Men with long hair and beards and ammunition bandoliers even came to the radio station. The long hairs were always drunk and as I was the only female at the radio station, the director assigned a guy to be my bodyguard. He was given a jeep to drive me back and forth because I often worked late at night.

The JNA commander was very professional and did not allow his soldiers to mix with the long hairs. In my contacts with the officers I could see they were ashamed of Četniks and of all the paramilitaries. The JNA was the fourth largest army in Europe with a long tradition, professional experience and educated officers.

Nobody in the JNA wanted to talk about the activities of Arkan or the others but they did nothing to stop them or to make them leave. In a way they performed parallel activities. Later when I spoke with Croats they would say, 'we prayed to god to be captured by the JNA and not the paramilitaries.' With the JNA they expected to be treated as POWs by international standards; while the others killed even Serbs who didn't agree with them.

Until 1993 when the UN arrived Vukovar was so isolated that we did not even have access to a shortwave radio. Then we opened a press center and we became available to the world media. This was a good opportunity for me because I met journalists from CNN, BBC, and everywhere. And finally it was possible for us to get information from the rest of the world.

Radio Dunav was the first civilian institution in Vukovar after the occupation. We never received military orders or censorship because no one was educated enough to censor us! But my goal was to create a serious, normal urban radio station and sometimes I did have conflicts with the Serb authorities.

On one occasion in 1992 we were allowed to accompany JNA generals to a UN-facilitated meeting with their Croat counterparts in a neutral town. After the meeting the Croat general invited the journalists into his office for refreshments and I wrote an article describing the general as very polite, a gentleman. For that, I was arrested. How dare I write that an 'Ustaša' was polite!

I was handcuffed and taken to a clandestine house in Vukovar. All the windows were covered with blankets. I was put in a room with a desk, a chair, a bed and a big lamp. It looked like something from the Gestapo. I was laughing! I was completely confused and couldn't believe this was happening.

An older man appeared and began to interrogate me. He told me he had been a Partisan and said in those days two of his comrades had been executed for stealing plums. He then accused me of working against the Serbs and said if I were a real Serb I wouldn't have written anything positive about an 'Ustaša.'

I suddenly realized that I had a really big problem and stopped laughing. He turned the lamp in my face to intimidate me. I tried to explain very carefully that I was a journalist and my intention was always to do balanced reporting. He was very angry. He left the room and turned the light off. I was alone in the dark for three hours.

Fortunately for me my director returned from a trip to Belgrade and vouched for me. The interrogator came back and warned me never to make the same mistake again.

A few minutes later another man entered with a document for me to sign that included an apology and a promise to be a good Serb. I was surprised and refused to sign. Another person came and told me my director 'strongly urged' me to sign. He was very worried. I could have been executed.

So I signed but that wasn't the end of it. I signed my name in Latin script as I had done all my life. The man came back so angry that he threw the papers in my face and shouted, 'You just signed that you are a good Serb and you signed in Latin!' So I signed again, in Cyrillic and was released.

I was threatened one more time when some high-ranking authorities decided I could not possibly be the editor-in-chief of the Serb radio station when my mother was Croat. Once again the director intervened and I wasn't bothered again.

The years of occupation were very hard for my mother as a Croat. She was subjected to taunts by Serbs but as a good wife she decided to stay with her husband. Even today she suffers the emotional consequences of that period. She was very hurt. After integration her old Croat friends returned but didn't want to talk to her because she had remained, so she fell into a symbolic hole without any reason or any way out.

I had lost touch with my boyfriend in July, before the war started. In mid-1992 I learned that he lost an arm in the fighting, that his mother had been dragged off a bus and executed and his brother killed. He and his father were captured and held in the Sremska Mitrovica concentration camp.

But I didn't know all that until later. One day early in December 1991 shortly after the radio station was inaugurated my staff and I went to the hospital to see what had happened there. In all the mess and terrible destruction I saw a stack of paper. My first thought was, 'oh, great, paper!' We didn't have any at that time. To my surprise I saw that the papers were documents, typed lists of all the wounded who had been admitted to the hospital. We started to read and suddenly I saw his name. He had been admitted at the end of October with gangrene in his right arm and it had been amputated.

I was very upset and wanted to know what had happened to him. I asked a JNA officer, an interrogator who was going to visit the concentration camp at Mitrovica to find out if he was there. The officer responded, 'Yes, he's there.' I asked if I could visit him and take some food. He laughed at me and said 'Are you completely crazy?' He added that all the prisoners were Ustaša and for my own good he would not tell anyone of my request.

I asked my director to help but he advised me to think very carefully about the consequences for me and my parents. As my mother was Croat, I just gave up.

Later, in 1992 I received a phone call as I was in the middle of a meeting with the JNA general in charge of the region. The phone was an old crank-style military apparatus connected only through Belgrade. I picked up the receiver and heard a voice say, 'Sanja, is that you? This is Zoran and I'm calling from Hungary.'

I was shocked but also frightened with the Serb general sitting next to me as I received a call from an 'Ustaša!' My legs turned to jelly and I had butterflies in my stomach. I was totally flustered. He said he had arrived in Hungary two days earlier after a prisoner exchange. Somehow he knew that I worked at the radio and managed to locate the number. He wanted me to join him in Hungary and asked me if I could find any information about his missing brother. I said it was impossible for me to travel but I would try to find out about his brother.

I searched for the brother for several years but was only able to discover that he had been wounded, had hidden in the Borovo Komerc shelter and was captured after the fall of Vukovar. His fate is still unknown and he is among the hundreds of missing.

My old boyfriend and I were able to meet years later. We had a long talk and today when we meet in town we stop and talk for a few minutes.

Even today I don't understand why all this happened. I simply accept that it happened to us and we all had a responsibility for it. And as life goes on after every tragedy, life just goes on.

The majority of the people still blame someone else. It is difficult to live with the awareness of guilt on your side, not just on someone else's. Serbs and Croats both have their own versions of how and why the war started but the reality is that Croatia wanted to separate and Serbia wouldn't allow that to happen. Belgrade and Zagreb generated everything.

Someone outside of Vukovar could say, 'Well, the locals didn't need to accept this,' but collective behavior is like lava, nothing can stop it.

In general the people of Vukovar don't talk about war crimes like Ovčara. At the time there were people on both sides who didn't know about these things but now, 15 years later, we have all learned about them. The problem is that each side protects its own nation so that those who committed the crimes are treated as heroes. If anyone says anything against those people the person is automatically accused of being a traitor.

For example as soon as there is evidence that either the Serb or Croat side committed a crime, the other side says, 'and what did you do to us?' It's much easier to point to someone else's guilt than to admit your own. 'If you hadn't, we wouldn't have,' and that's the beginning and end of the story.

When the integration process began in 1998 the saying was, 'Croats and Serbs do not have to be friends but do have to live together.' This is still true. Serbs and Croats work together in almost every institution in Vukovar from cultural and governmental offices to the hospitals and schools. We socialize, we even go out together, but we never discuss the so-called "closed stories" of the war.

SHE WOULD NEVER INVITE ME TO HER HOUSE, NOR WOULD I INVITE HER TO MINE
D.H. 2010

I was born in Štitar, a Croat village with two or three Serb families. My father was Slovak. After secondary school I went to Zagreb to study food technology but didn't like it. My best friends at that time were very mixed: Croat, Serb and Macedonian. From 1981-1989 I rented a room in Zagreb from an actress who was a Partisan during the war. I remember that once we saw Milosević giving a speech on TV and she said, 'there is going to be a war.' I didn't understand at the time, really no one did.

There was some kind of war in Slovenia but no one thought it would happen here. There were so-called 'incidents' around Croatia, in Knin, in Plitviče and then in Borovo Selo on May 2nd. By July we were seeing things on TV but we didn't believe it was going to be war.

On July 2nd a friend from my village was killed in Mirkovci. He was in the ZNG and was shot in action. I realize now that for me, the war started then.

After November 1991 my brother joined the Tigers, the first professional brigade of the Croatian army. He was killed in 1993 near Dubrovnik.

I decided to get serious about my studies and transferred to the Faculty of History. I received my Master's Degree in 2000 and started teaching in Vukovar in 2001.

It was a big shock to come here. It was not my territory but I felt a moral obligation to come and help. Vukovar was a symbol of suffering and I had friends who had suffered.

For the first time in my life I heard people who were not speaking Croatian. I lived in Mitnica where there were many Serbs and I felt I had to be careful how I spoke.
Croats avoided talking about problems; they avoided any painful conversation because they didn't want Serbs to see their pain and they wanted to avoid conflict. In those first years when

I worked with Serbs they did not accept Croatia as a separate country; they behaved as though it was still Yugoslavia.

I have taught at the high school for ten years. For the past nine years it has been a mixed school in the sense that Croats and Serbs attend the same sessions, but not the same classes. They do mix in other activities like music and sports. I teach History in Croatian. Serb kids study Croatian History with Serb teachers and they study Serb history 30% of the time.

In the first years I taught the war in a very simple way, without emotion because some of the kids had been victims and it was difficult for them. I do say 'Serb aggressors' because the media says that and I believe it is true.

The conflicts in the school are not political, just kids fighting. They use 'politics' as an excuse but it's not real. I see them in the streets later talking with no problem.

The children don't like to study. The families have many social and economic problems and there is little communication between parents and children. Most of the kids do graduate however. Many of the Croats go to the coast to study tourism and some go to the University of Osijek. Most of the Serb kids go to Serbia to continue their studies.

I don't think there will be school integration. The economic situation is not good and teachers are afraid of losing their jobs.

There is good professional communication and cooperation among all the teachers. We are professionals and we want to improve our school. My relations with most of the Serb teachers are good but there are some who won't say hello.

I do talk with one of the Serb teachers about the students and we help each other out, but we avoid any talk about the war. She would never invite me to her house nor would I invite her to my house. We can have coffee together in school but not outside. This is not important to me; the important thing is the work.

The students seem to be more interested in the war now than they were before. Perhaps because for them it was a long time ago. They're interested but they don't want the town to become a museum. They just fantasize they will go away somewhere to make a lot of money without a lot of work!

WE WERE DEFENDING ALL THOSE WHO STAYED IN VUKOVAR
Z.K. 2007

I have lived most of my life in Vukovar. I was 35 in 1991, married with two children, working as a car mechanic. I was always Croat.

We began organizing secretly in late 1990. It was obvious by then that after HDZ won the elections we wouldn't be allowed to leave Yugoslavia peacefully. Weapons had been going to the villages from Serbia since early that year; they had Thompsons and Kalashnikovs. By February 1991 the Serbs were establishing barricades around their villages and we were doing the same in ours. Bogdanovci was Croat but otherwise Vukovar was surrounded by Serb villages. We were given orders from Zagreb when to set up or remove barricades. We always followed orders from the police chief in Zagreb.

All Serb children were evacuated from Vukovar in late May at the end of the school term. Everyone was just waiting for war. We knew about the Serb evacuations and did the same thing in July. We organized a trip to the seaside for about 1000 kids with the assistance of the Red Cross. There were 15 or 20 busloads of kids. In August they wanted to return because the situation was so quiet. So I went to get my children and just ten days later the war started.

None of us really believed war was certain; we were afraid it was coming but didn't really believe it. There were only about 2000 defenders during the entire siege and just a few hundred were prepared in any way. We were all just ordinary people. I didn't even know how to dismantle a gun! I think it was fear that saved us because later when I was captured and interrogated, they wanted to know where I got my training. Where? I never had any training. They couldn't believe that such a small group of us, really only a handful with any training, could have mounted a resistance.

The war started on August 24th. At that time there were about 25,000 people in Vukovar and we had no idea the war would start that day. I was the commander in Mitnica. At 3:00 pm a column of 15 tanks came toward Vukovar but the road was mined so they turned off but then a plane flew over and rocketed our barricade. We flew in every direction! That was our baptism of fire.

They could have taken us then. We only had about 200 defenders in Mitnica, and just ten Kalashnikovs, ten semi-automatics, 20 or 30 shotguns and one surface-to-air missile. We had three Motorolas for communication and there were only 15 Motorolas in all of Vukovar. We couldn't have stopped them. Meanwhile the JNA troops were being told '10,000 Ustaša are defending Vukovar,' and other propaganda.

Even the next day, August 25th we didn't know it was war. None of us expected it to be so fierce and so disastrous. We still thought Europe or America would say 'enough' and stop it. The only thing we knew was that it was our town. We had nowhere to go so we had to stay and defend our town.

From August 25th to November 18th there was constant shelling from rockets, aerial bombs, artillery, war ships on the Danube, airplanes and tanks. There were a few attempts to occupy Mitnica but they never managed to take even one house. There were about 450-550 people still in Mitnica during that time.

On October 2nd the last road out of Vukovar was cut. That was the end of any access. By November we could see that things were going from bad to worse and no help was going to arrive from outside, no support. We decided we had to start negotiations.

On the evening of November 17th we were invited to a meeting with Colonel Popović of the JNA who is now on trial in the Hague for crimes in Kosovo. He sent us a message by Motorola and we accepted. Three of us agreed to meet with him at Goldschmitts, the manor house on the south side of town on the 18th. We told him our demands: an International Red Cross representative as witness to the surrender and a firm cease fire. Everything was quiet that night.

We met at around noon on the 18th and reached an agreement that the civilians would be transported to Croatia and that the defenders would surrender all weapons, with guarantees for their safety. All would be sent to a POW camp for future prisoner exchange. I agreed to make a list of everyone to hand over.

By the 17th downtown Vukovar was occupied by JNA and Četniks. The hospital was taken on the 18th-19th and Mitnica at noon on the 18th. All of us, civilians and defenders, had to go to the center of town and then everyone – maybe 5-6000 people walked to the cemetery. The civilians were taken to Serbia and later released.

We were 184 defenders. We surrendered our weapons and were taken to the metal sheds at Ovčara overnight. That is where we suffered the worst abuse, at the hands of the local Serbs who said they were going to 'plow us under the ground.' We overheard arguments between the Serb paramilitaries and the JNA over who would have control of us. The Četniks wanted us but the JNA refused. The next day we were put on busses for Sremska Mitrovica concentration camp.

The rest of those who came to Ovčara after we left - all the people from the hospital - were killed. We believe about 300 were massacred there.

My group of 184 was safe. I was held in the camp for nine months; some were released earlier. I was in solitary confinement. We were beaten, forced to eat tablespoonfuls of salt, and then not given anything to drink, and so on. There were about 1000 of us in the camp, men, women and children, including ten women defenders. Most were released fairly quickly and after nine months everyone was exchanged.

Our spirit was so strong throughout. We weren't just defending our own homes but also the people who had stayed in the houses and basements of Vukovar.

I stayed in the army until Operation Storm and then left. I returned to Vukovar in 1998.

I LOVE MY TOWN AND MY PEOPLE AND I NEVER DID ANYTHING WRONG
A.V. 2010

I am very happy that someone has asked to talk to me. I am pleased to have the opportunity to tell the truth.

I was born in Vukovar and lived in Šajmište. My parents worked at the Borovo factory; my father was a manager and my mother worked on the shoe assembly line as a section chief with fifty people under her direction. About 25,000 people from everywhere worked in Borovo at that time.

I went to school in Vukovar and then to Osijek to study electronics. However, my family didn't have money, so I returned to Vukovar and later went to flying school and then to parachute training. I earned high marks and wanted to go to the military school for officers, but only a few people from all of Yugoslavia could be selected. So eventually I joined the Special Forces of the JNA.

When I was growing up my two best friends were Croats. We grew up together and didn't know who was what. We had no problems in high school. One of my friends died in the war; the other one came to visit me ten years ago. That was my first visit after integration. He said, 'if my friends knew I was here they would kill me!' His cousin was my first love from 1986-88.

The first time I noticed problems was in 1990. That spring I went to see my girlfriend. A Croat guy on the street said, 'You're not welcome here.' Then we went to the Quo Vadis club and they wouldn't let me in. My girlfriend protested saying, 'He's my boyfriend,' but they refused. She explained to me that 'her guys' wanted to make their own country. When we left the club they shouted, 'Daria, you can come back but not him.' I thought it was just a kid thing.

Two months later I was with my girlfriend in Mitnica. Some guys were standing on the corner representing a kind of line where Serbs couldn't pass. They wouldn't let me cross the line.

Things started happening in the town. We couldn't go to Croat bars without getting beaten up. There weren't any uniforms around yet but I know who was doing what. Some people in Mitnica were paying kids to put bombs in Serb kiosks - the ones with Cyrillic writing.

Even in 1990 you could see Croatian flags everywhere and signs like 'We will kill all Serbs' and 'Serbs not welcome here.' Things started getting serious. I joined the JNA to do my military service and had Special Forces training in Niš. My parents stayed behind believing everything would be okay.

On September 1st, 1990 I came home on leave and met my brother in the train station in Vinkovci as he was leaving for the army in Kosovo. I had my uniform on. We went to have a drink near the station and were told 'You're not welcome here.'

In the army we were all friends. No one was talking nationalism then. I became an instructor in the Parachute School and I remember they told me I should stay there, warning me, 'there will be a war in your town soon.'

For me the war started in 1990. I felt we were not welcome here. Before that I didn't know what I was. My family was always Yugoslavian.

I got out of the army in March 1991. When I came home my family and friends were okay. Croats asked me why I had been in the army and I told them I was just doing my military service.

By May there were barricades in the villages. Serb people were not able to go to work anymore. They were frightened. We all heard that some people were being kidnapped and tortured.

May 25th, 1991 was my girlfriend's birthday and that was my last day not in hiding. I hid for one month; even my parents didn't know where I was but I let them know I was okay. Then after a month I crossed the Danube.

My father disappeared on September 1st and we still don't know what happened to him. He was a volunteer for the Red Cross in those days, delivering food to elderly people. At that time it was dangerous to go outside. He usually delivered food in the early morning or late afternoon. He took food to an old grandmother here in the center of Vukovar. She was the last person who saw him.

We reported his disappearance to the Croatian and Serbian Red Cross. An international organization for missing people came to get information about his disappearance. My grandmother and I gave DNA samples to them. I continue looking for information today.

After that my family left for Montenegro and I returned to Šid to rejoin the army. I did it 50% for my grandmother and 50% because I had been kicked out of town and wanted to do something about it.

By October 1st I was back here fighting in the forest, in the Territorial Defense. I was wounded by a mine on October 13th.

The war robbed me of my youth. I was wounded six times. After the first time I said, 'that's the last time I will pick up a gun' but then my brother was killed and I went back. I lost my brother, my father, and my uncle in the war.

I was in the military hospital in Serbia on November 18th and returned to Vukovar on November 21st. It was terrible, terrible, in ruins. The smell of death was everywhere. They were picking up bodies in the streets and loading them on carts. They were just bodies, Serb or Croat. There was no water or electricity. People collected snow for drinking water. There wasn't any food. The streets were full of animals – pigs and dogs. There were parrots in the trees that had been indoor pets.

My house was okay but totally empty; everything had been stolen.

It was a scene of death everywhere. Then the snow came and covered the smell until spring, when once again you could smell death and rotted food.

The JNA was in Vukovar along with the Territorial Defense and Arkan with his people. I stayed six months. I helped my artist friend take art from the museum to Serbia to keep it safe. We found a Croat military hospital in the tunnels under the museum.

I kept looking for information about my father and that is how I first heard something about Ovčara in 1992. I only heard that some people had been killed there. No one knew about what happened at the hospital and I only heard because I was searching for my father and was close to people who knew.

I joined the Special Forces and fought in Croatia and Bosnia for three years. I never hurt anyone innocent.

I returned to Vukovar in 1995 and started to work. It was very hard here. There was no money in the town and people were barely surviving. There were some Croats here at that time. My mother was working in a canteen, a job her Croat friend got for her.

Now I have a Croat wife! We were the first mixed marriage in Vukovar after 1991!

It was hard to accept Vukovar would be part of Croatia then. Four out of six Serbs left with the integration because they were afraid. Croats returned and took back their houses. I stayed because I am not afraid of anyone. I love my town and my people and I never did anything wrong.

I was never addicted to war. For most of us we fought because the media was presenting us as the aggressors. I didn't have any desire to kill anyone. I was there because everyone hated us.

I have PTSD, of course. A doctor diagnosed it, but I decided not to have him sign the paper because that diagnosis can affect your work and your life. But I drink too much and I have nightmares. I never sleep more than four hours. I try to control all this. I have two kids, nine and eleven years old, and I don't want it to affect them.

We were eligible for pensions from Serbia but I donated mine for poor children there; it was only 80 Euros and they need it more than I do. My mom gets 250 Euros for my brother and she goes to Serbia every month to collect it.

There haven't been any revenge killings here, no violence of that sort. And if there were the police would react immediately. People were forced to go to war and they are sick of it, both sides.

My children know there was a war. I explained to them who they are. They know they wouldn't exist if I hadn't decided to stay here. I could have ended up in Serbia or Montenegro and wouldn't have married their mother!

I tell them they should never be ashamed of who they are. They are Orthodox. We are Serbs living in Croatia. I respect my wife's beliefs, but she knew when we married in 1997 how it would be.

Now my friends and I realize the war was all started by politicians. They didn't care about the people.

Thank you for asking me about this. No one ever asked me these questions. You should know the truth.

NOTHING ABOUT THE WAR IS CERTAIN EXCEPT THE NUMBER OF DEAD AND WOUNDED
Z.T. 2006/2010

I was born in Vukovar and lived my entire life here except during the war and occupation. My parents were also born here and worked in the Borovo factory. My brother and I worked there at various times also. Borovo was the largest employer in the region with some 23,000 employees of more than two dozen nationalities.

My father was a member of the Communist Party and always behaved as a Communist. He told me 'first of all you are a Yugoslav, then a teacher, then a Croat.' On every religious holiday we had traditional food and customs but that had to be secret or you were not a 'good communist.' Religion was never forbidden but if you wanted to work in a public institution you had to think about your children's future also.

In grammar school we were taught to think globally. We always looked West. The U.S. was a goddess for us; we saw America as keeping us safe from Russia. Tito was a tightrope walker.

We all participated in party youth groups. You carried your party membership card with your driver's license in case you were stopped. You showed it 'accidentally' and the police would give you a lecture but no ticket.

Life was better then, at least for the common people. The average family could afford a car, a flat, all the necessities. Education was free and I think over 50% of high school graduates went to university.

In 1985 I was working for Borovo when a friend offered me a better job. I thought about leaving and talked to my father. He said, 'Think of this. Borovo is a Yugoslav factory so when Yugoslavia collapses, Borovo collapses and vice-versa.' He was right.

In Yugoslavia we were all equal but Serbs were just a bit more equal. In 1988 I was in a bar with a Serb friend who told me that in order to succeed it was not important to have a degree, but 'it IS important to be a Serb.' Croatia wanted independence and the fall of the Berlin Wall signaled it was time for new arrangements. Serbia had always dominated and felt superior with its religious myths and legends. By the late 70s and early 80s even my father was a little disappointed. He said the 'Serbian bourgeoisie dominates.'

The war happened because Serbia wanted to dominate and Croatia wanted to separate.

There were no problems for Serbs here until after May 2nd. However they started building barricades in 1990 and blocked off Vukovar for six months. My friends and I - Serbs and Croats - would be sitting together asking what is going on here? Is everyone crazy?

From December 1990 on Serb paramilitaries were going to the Serb villages to protect and arm the people. But I still didn't believe there was any possibility of war here. I thought the JNA would never allow it. Then one day a JNA tank appeared in downtown Vukovar with a soldier at the machine gun ready to fire. That was even before May. There was already a lot of tension.

In the spring of 1991 I saw 'Četniks', big bearded men with bandoliers and American Thompson machineguns, in a bar outside Vukovar.

The population of Vukovar at that time was 44,000 in town, 88,000 in the country. According to the 1990 census it was 44% Croat, 37% Serb, the rest minorities or "Yugoslav." Before 1990 national identity was unimportant.

But by June 1991 your politics became unimportant, your religion unimportant. It was all about national identity and here there were only two sides - Croat and Serb - and both sides demanded loyalty: Are you with us or against us? Are you ready to fight? My friends and I discussed all this but still none of us thought about war. I didn't believe it when one Serb friend joined the radical SDS but he told me it was because of pressure. The only way for any of us to stay uninvolved was to flee. If just one American tank had appeared, nothing would have happened.

I left on July 17th. My wife was eight months pregnant. There were shootings outside town but I didn't really think of leaving until a friend offered us a house on Hvar in the Adriatic so we left for a month. In August I called friends both Serb and Croat in Vukovar and they said not to come back. My Serb friend said big attacks were planned on the police station.

Radio Vukovar was broadcast all over Croatia so we had news. On September 15th they called for volunteers to come and fight. One friend of mine went but called me two weeks later back in Zagreb. He had entered and left Vukovar by the Corn Way, through the cornfields. He said 'only the insane and dead are there.' His mother lived just a few kilometers from downtown but it took him four hours to get there: running and lying down, running and lying down through the gunfire.

My father left on August 15th. My wife and I went to Zagreb and I started a little business. Eventually we bought a house there. I came to visit Vukovar in 1998 and moved back in 2002.

Things have changed dramatically for the better since 2002. At that time Serbs and Croats could not be seen together talking in public. But recently, I took my friends, Serb and Croat, to my brother's café and no one reacted. I have never heard of any revenge killings since I returned and none are listed in police records.

My Serb friends and I can talk about things without getting angry. We are aware we don't have the same opinions so we just don't go too deep. They say that the crimes committed after the fall of Vukovar were all about revenge and were committed by local Serbs and paramilitary, that it's about World War II revenge and collective memory.

Both religions demand forgiveness but the strongest believers are the least forgiving.

Still I can't believe it happened. There is not one single family in Vukovar that didn't have a friend or relative on the other side. One Serb friend said, 'I don't want to shoot at you or your family! Do you want to shoot me or my family?' No crimes can be justified on either side. The question is how to move on.

2010

Recently I had an experience with a six-year old boy in my language class. He was showing off his fighting skills and I told him to stop because he could hurt someone. He said, 'I am the strongest one here and I can beat up the Croat kids.' I said, 'yes you could but then their fathers will come and beat you up and your father will come to beat them up and then there is a big war.'

The little boy said, 'yes, but we will invite the Serbs to come and beat them all.' I was shocked and decided to just end it there. They get this from Serb TV and from their parents and grandparents.

On both sides you still have about 30% who live in the war zone, who don't want to accept the situation. It is impossible to change them.

I SAID I WILL GO WHERE THE COFFEE IS GOOD
AND THERE I WILL SIT
Z.S. 2010

I was born in Vukovar in 1954. Between us my wife and I have four children. I worked in the Borovo factory as an engineer until the war started; I had trained as an electrical engineer and we provided the last source of energy during the war.

Before the war more than 20 nationalities lived in Vukovar. The beauty of this town was its multi-ethnicity. At that time it was impossible to imagine that the politics started by Slobodan Milosević in 1988-89 could have such influence on our town and all of Croatia. Our families would get together for holidays and birthdays and talk politics but no one could imagine that in just days we would be shooting at each other. Even as we watched the problems in Romania with Ceaucescu on TV, sitting in our warm, comfortable homes, we could not imagine it would happen to us.

In March of 1991 people from outside Vukovar - from Serbia - were coming to the villages forcing people to take weapons. The workers in Borovo were not paid for six months; 90% of the management was Serb and they were telling the workers not to strike, saying the HDZ was making the wage problem political. The European and Russian markets were down and, since we were Socialist, all the money went through Belgrade. Someone there knew war was coming and stopped sending money.

We had always been the second wealthiest town in Yugoslavia; we had a high standard of living here. But when people have economic problems they are easily divided, creating conditions for war. Politicians used the economic situation to prepare the groundwork for war.

In the villages the Serbs built barricades and told people not to go to work at Borovo because of the 'Ustaša.' Somebody very carefully organized what was happening, to create "Greater Serbia." In Serbia the media propaganda told the people they were not welcome here and if they came they would be tortured.

There was a referendum in Croatia and 98% voted for independence. Milosević said, 'if you want your independence we will take parts of your country.'

The summer of 1991 was almost an ordinary summer here in Vukovar. Families and kids went to the coast on holiday. I was working that summer and even though the events of May 2nd were just three kilometers from my home I still thought politicians would solve the problems. We all continued to work and lead normal lives, though by then we knew that people in the villages were being armed, and after May 2nd, Croats also began to arm themselves.

During the war I stayed at the factory and maintained the generator. I was a soldier until November 20th, 1991. I was in the last group of 5000, taken to the concentration camp in Niš and then to Begejći. I was a prisoner for 76 days and suffered serious injuries from beatings, including broken bones. In Niš a JNA officer named Radulozić was responsible for the tortures; in Begejći it was the JNA and paramilitaries. None of them have been brought to trial for war crimes. For years Serbia would never admit the existence of the camps.

We were released and I went to Rijeka to join my family. We had to wait seven years for the return. The economic situation was very difficult for us and I had to go to Austria to work illegally, doing the hardest jobs like construction. The Austrian police caught me in 1996 and I went back to Rijeka.

I finally returned to Vukovar on January 13, 1998. The city was destroyed and there was lots of work for all of us to rebuild our homes, the schools and everything. The return of the refugees was very slow because it depended on reconstruction. I finished rebuilding my house in August 1999 and brought my family back to Vukovar.

Then I went back to the university. My daughter was feeling very lost in her life and didn't know what to do. I suggested she study theology and I promised I would study with her. So she did, and I did, and I graduated at the top of the class!

I was vice-president of the organization that helped refugees return and then president of the SDP, Social Democratic Party. I decided to run for mayor because the other parties, both Croat and Serb were based on nationalism and didn't work for the community. In 2009 I received 52% of the vote for a four-year term.

One of the first things I did after the election was to go to a Croat café with three Serb staff members to show the town that everything in Vukovar belongs to everyone. I sat there for one hour so everyone could see that Serbs are welcome. Suddenly ten Croats came to sit and talk to the Serbs and to me! This was an important sign to the people. The previous mayors had spied on who was who and what they were doing and who went to which café. I said I will go to where the coffee is good and there I will sit. This was a message to the entire town.

Now it is clear that people are free to go everywhere. Before, only Croats went to the concerts but now all can go. Last winter we had an ice skating rink and everyone was enjoying it, talking, skating together – and no guns.

As mayor I am in control of the budget. I control who gets money for what. Before this administration the money was not spent correctly but now I can be certain where it's going. Investors from outside know that this mayor is not corrupt and doesn't take any 'percentages' off their investments.

Vukovar is now in a better financial situation than any other town in the country. We don't owe money to anyone and there is no deficit for the first time ever. We have projects from the EU and towns all over the country send solidarity money for reconstruction.

But young people leave because of the economic situation. Before the war there were more jobs than people but now there is no industry and there are more people than jobs. We need investment and jobs to keep them here.

The best thing I have been able to accomplish so far is to send 600 kids and their families on a free holiday to the coast and to provide scholarships for 106 students to university. And nationality had nothing to do with the selection of participants.

I don't know if I will run for mayor again. There is a lot of pressure against me from the other parties. They accuse me of things I have never done and honestly I never imagined the human mind could sink to such depths. I pray that god will give me enough strength to continue.

Made in the USA
Charleston, SC
03 October 2011